D1627649

THE ANCIENT WORLD

EGYPT AND THE OLD TESTAMENT

EGYPT AND THE OLD TESTAMENT

BY

T. ERIC PEET

Brunner Professor of Egyptology in the University of Liverpool;
formerly Craven Fellow in the University of Oxford

LIVERPOOL
THE UNIVERSITY PRESS OF LIVERPOOL LTD.
LONDON
HODDER AND STOUGHTON LTD.
MCMXXII.

Made and Printed in Great Britain
C. TINLING & CO., LTD., 53, Victoria Street, Liverpool, and at London and Prescot

PREFACE

YET another book on Egypt and the Bible! It might have been thought that all that is worth saying on the subject had been said, and well said. This would be a mistake. Each year some fresh discovery modifies our conception of Egypt and its history, and it is not a rare event for a belief which no one ever thought of questioning to be destroyed by a single blow of the excavator's pick.

Perhaps no portion of Egyptian history has been more brightly illumined by the discoveries of the last ten years than that into which the sojourn of the Israelites in Egypt and the exodus must have fallen. It is therefore no unsuitable time to put into words free, as far as possible, from the technicalities of the excavator and the philologist the bearing of the latest finds in Egypt on the narrative of the Old Testament.

It is not, however, without a feeling of anxiety that an archaeologist enters the much trodden field of biblical criticism, for many whose good-will and opinion he values still feel a traditional resentment at any attempt to treat the biblical narrative like any other ancient document, and to expose it to the full light of modern discovery. Such as these may refuse to compromise with archaeology and philology, and their attitude is at least consistent. If, however, these sciences are to be consulted at all let it be done honestly. If they are to be quoted when they support the Bible story they should also be faced when they contradict it. And above all things, let their evidence be produced in its original form, and not twisted and perverted by being taken out of its context and clothed in question-begging epithets. Let it not be forgotten, moreover, that the great masters of thirty and forty years ago in these sciences have been succeeded by a younger generation of scholars, who, starting from the foundations which their predecessors laid, and benefiting by ever accumulating discoveries and improved methods of research, have reached results which, in many cases, do not agree with those of the older band, and which nevertheless can be proved to be correct.[1]

There are writers, too, both among excavators and among biblical students who, in their anxiety to prove, by means of archaeology, the accuracy

[1] Numerous writers on the relations of archaeology and the Bible are either unacquainted with, or purposely ignore, the work of such masters as Griffith, Gardiner, Reisner, Sethe, Erman, Dévaud and Lacau.

of the Bible narrative, display a zeal which proves their own undoing. They make identifications of place-names which can be shown to be incorrect or at least unjustifiable, and in some cases they go so far as to make statements with regard to Egyptian history and religion which any serious student knows to be inaccurate. Such writers, instead of vindicating the narrative of the Old Testament, merely discredit it by a disingenuousness which is bound in the end to be exposed. The truth is that there is in Egypt singularly little evidence which bears directly on the Bible narrative. This does not indicate that that narrative is false, for even greater historical events have taken place in Egypt and left practically no traces. Those who are anxious to vindicate the Old Testament story would do well to realize this, and to perceive that to distort or falsify facts in order to bring them into connection with the sojourn or the exodus can do nothing but harm to the cause they seek to defend.

My thanks are due to the Rev. L. W. Grensted, Principal of Egerton Hall, Manchester, with whom I have discussed many points connected with this volume. My indebtedness to Dr. A. H. Gardiner's recent researches on Delta geography will be obvious to every reader.

CONTENTS

                                                              PAGE
PREFACE   5

CHAPTER

I   NATURE AND VALUE OF BIBLICAL TRADITION   11

II   EARLY RELATIONS OF EGYPT AND PALESTINE   37

III ABRAM'S DESCENT INTO EGYPT   47

IV   THE SOJOURN IN EGYPT   64

V   THE EXODUS   105

VI   SOLOMON, JEROBOAM AND ASA   146

VII SO AND TIRHAKAH   167

VIII NECHO AND THE PROPHET JEREMIAH   .   .   180

IX   THE JEWISH COLONIES IN EGYPT   .   .   .   189

X   THE EPISODE OF ONIAS   209

BIBLIOGRAPHY   229

INDEX   231

Two Maps at end of volume

1. THE NEAR AND MIDDLE EAST.

2. THE GEOGRAPHY OF THE EXODUS.

CHAPTER I

THE contents of the first few books of the Old Testament form the most considerable mass of tradition which has, so far as we know at present, survived from the ancient world. That it has so survived is due to two causes. In the first place the Jewish people has been endowed with a sense of nationality to which there is perhaps no parallel in history; this has enabled it not only to survive but also to preserve its records. In the second place the fact that Christianity was grafted on to the Jewish religion has resulted in the embodiment of Jewish tradition in the literature of Christianity and in its consequent survival.

The connection of this tradition with our religion for a long time protected it, for better or for worse, from criticism of every kind. In the last century, however, the rise of the sciences of geology and physics gradually showed that a literal interpretation of the legends of the creation and the flood was impossible. A little later the development of archaeology began to make it clear that even some of the later episodes of the Pentateuch could not be accepted in their literal form, while the study of anthropology, folklore, ancient history and comparative religion showed that Hebrew tradition was not something unique in its formation and structure, but followed much the same lines as that of other ancient peoples.

But when we proceed to ask what these lines are we at once find ourselves face to face with a difficulty, for the subject is one regarding which the keenest controversy at present rages among anthropologists. To an age which took all traditions for historical fact succeeded one which regarded them all as baseless fairy tales, or at the best as a series of astral or nature myths.

> "So, I bent brow o'er *Prolegomena*.
> And, after Wolf, a dozen of his like
> Proved there was never any Troy at all,
> Neither Besiegers nor Besieged,—nay, worse,—
> No actual Homer, no authentic text,
> No warrant for the fiction I, as fact,
> Had treasured in my heart and soul so long."

This view was directly antipodal to that which it displaced, and, as usual in such cases, a partial reaction was inevitable. The present attitude towards the problem of more sober critics as typified by such a scholar as Farnell may be rapidly summed up as follows.

The most fruitful classification of myth, used in its widest sense to include " all the various forms of unattested oral tradition that we distinguish from written history," is according to the sources from which they are or may reasonably be supposed to be derived. " Two leading divisions emerge clearly, on the one hand nature-myths, referring to the phenomena of the heavens, the earth and the waters ; and on the other hand myths that we may call human or social, including stories concerning ritual, the origin of social institutions and culture, wars, raids, hunting, the movements of peoples, the prowess of indivi-duals." The tendency of a certain school of thought has been to assign practically all myth to the former of these classes. Thus Penelope is stated to have been originally a water-fowl of Arcadia, and Odysseus her husband a year-daemon. Now though there are doubtless cases where a myth at first sight human eventually rests on some fact in nature, yet the indiscriminate assigning of all myth to such sources fails to reckon with the fact that the main interest of savage conversation, and therefore of oral tradition, is not so much the course of regular nature as the irregular course of human action. Moreover, to assign a myth full of complex and curious detail to a " natural " origin is not to explain it, but to make it far more incomprehensible than before ; the assumption that Amphiaraos of Boeotia and Argos was the daemon of a lake does not in the least explain the curious events of his career. In some cases it is abundantly clear that the myth arose in precisely the opposite way to that postulated here, and that tales which originally had a purely human origin and bearing have in course of time received the addition of a nature element. " We might," says Farnell, " establish it as a rule of sanity never to interpret a myth as a nature-myth if the human social explanation lies nearer to hand."

Passing from true nature-myths to the human and social class, we may notice that these group themselves conveniently into three sub-classes : firstly religious and ritual, dealing chiefly with the relations of gods and men, and the origins of religious observances and ceremonies ; secondly, sociological myths, which explain the origins of culture, generally centring in the person of a hero ; and thirdly, historic myths, dealing with wars and migrations of peoples and the exploits of individual men. Since the history of an early people is very frequently that of its protecting deities, religious myth will often contain a considerable amount of history proper. On the other hand it has long been recognized that ritual is itself a frequent source of myth, a story being invented in order to furnish an explanation for a custom or ritual whose true origin has been forgotten. The Feast of the Passover is an excellent instance of this. It is certainly older than the time of the exodus, in fact there are reasons for supposing it to be very primitive indeed in origin. Before the eighth century B.C. its origin had been lost, but was restored by a method well known to all students of ancient religion, that of a pun or play upon words. Its unintelligible name *pesaḥ* was explained as a derivation from *pāsaḥ* "to pass over," and made to refer to the Lord's passing over the houses of the Israelites when He smote the first-born of the Egyptians. The tenth plague was also employed to explain one of the central features of the Passover, namely the smearing of blood on lintels and side-posts, a custom of immense antiquity in the East. The whole forms an instructive example of the methods of the Hebrew folklorists.

The second type of human myth, the socio-logical, is of value in that it may reasonably be expected to preserve some nucleus of true information concerning the social organization of the people among which it arose. Yet in using myths for this purpose extreme caution is necessary, for it is always to be borne in mind that myth is apt to form not round what is normal but what is abnormal in human action, and that thus a myth which appears to contain an instance of, for example, matriarchal succession, may prove, not that this was the rule, but rather that it was the exception in the society where the myth took its rise.

With regard to the third type of human myth, that which deals with events purporting to be historic, the modern attitude may be summed up in Farnell's words. " There has come in recent years, to aid both our sanity and our science, the conviction that the most potent cause of the type of myths just referred to has been actual reality or historic matter of fact." Chadwick's researches have shown that much of the content of the great Teutonic saga has a historical background, and it is probable that the same will eventually prove to be true of the Greek. The detail may be and probably is mostly incorrect, but the underlying basis of fact is true in many cases, and, surprising as this may seem at first sight, there seems to be good reason for believing that the personal names are often historical.

When we come to apply these principles to the contents of the Old Testament it is at once apparent that these consist of material of very various nature and value, which can, however, for practical purposes, be divided into three heads.

Under the first head, the prehistoric, we may class the whole of the narrative down to the beginning of the patriarchal period, including of course the narratives of the creation and the flood. The remarkable Sumerian and Babylonian parallels which have been recently discovered to both these legends show that here we are dealing with a tradition so ancient as to be common to the Hebrews and their eastern neighbours in Mesopotamia. Historically these stories are probably almost valueless ; they merely show us the mind of primitive man reflecting on his own origin and on that of the universe. The names of Adam and Eve are simply the Hebrew words for " man " and " life " respectively. If there ever took place an event which gave rise to the flood story—and there are scholars who still find this the simplest way of accounting for the legend—it has left no other trace in history, and in the

B

Hebrew account as it has come down to us it occurs in suspicious company, for it is closely bound up with two myths which were clearly invented, the one to explain diversity of language, and the other to provide an origin for the rainbow.

Under the second head, the semi-historic, we may place the story of the patriarchs. Here the principles which have been enunciated above for the appraisement of the value of myth must be rigorously applied. There is no contemporary written evidence for the period, and the compilers of the earliest documents embodied in Genesis and Exodus, those known as J and E, probably had before them little more than an oral tradition already handed down through many centuries and suffering from all the defects inherent in such a tradition. While it undoubtedly contains in its general lines certain historical truths, yet its detail, added at various periods, may be regarded as of most doubtful value, and in some cases it would be unwise to accept even the main outlines without very careful sifting of evidence.

Strangely enough. the adherents of the extreme astral or nature school in mythology have devoted but little time to the myths of the Old Testament, which might have been expected to provide them with a happy hunting ground. It is true that a few writers, as for example Jensen, have attempted to show the astral origin of much of the pre-patriarchal legend, but they have not extended their attempt into the domain of patriarchal story. Here we have undoubtedly myth of the second main class, the human and social. Each of the three sub-divisions of that class is well represented. The history of the Hebrew people is that of their god, and for this reason the large portion of their myth which is directly connected with their god and their religion may be expected to contain much historical truth. On the other hand, one of the documents on which the present compilation of the Pentateuch is founded, that known as P, is the work of a priestly school mainly bent on explaining the origin of its ritual and ceremonies ; we must therefore expect cases where the desire to explain an observance is the father of the myth. In the attempt to glean information about the state of society among the early Hebrews from myths of the sociological type it will be necessary to keep constantly in mind that what the legend has recorded is less often the obvious and normal than the unusual and abnormal, and that what might at first sight appear to be a custom embedded in a story is often not a custom but a breach of it.

And finally, we must be prepared to find that much of the biblical myth does actually record the deeds and prowess of historical races and persons, wrapped up, no doubt, in a mass of incorrect detail. Never must we lose sight of the axiom that the most probable reason for the existence of a story which is not palpably a nature-myth, or an explanation of an existing custom or practice, is that the thing actually happened. What has been said with regard to the probable correctness of personal names in myth must also be borne in mind. The patriarchal narrative is rich in such names. It is true that many of these are quite clearly names of tribes and not of persons. Keturah, for instance, is spoken of as Abram's second wife (Gen. 25.1), but her sons and grandsons are represented as tribes (Gen. 25.2-4), and Genesis is full of such examples. At the same time any attempt to explain the patriarchs as exclusively tribes rather than individuals brings in its train a host of difficulties, and the possibility that individuals of importance in Hebrew history named Isaac and Jacob really existed should not be lightly dismissed, even though we are not prepared to credit all the stories which cluster about their names or to believe that the one lived 180 years and the other 147.

It is interesting for the purpose of this book to apply these considerations to the story of the sojourn in Egypt. The exact value of its detail is judged differently by different scholars, and it will be seen in the sequel that much of it can be shown to be later than the events themselves. But, with regard to the main fact that at some time or other certain of the people who subsequently came to be known as the Hebrews dwelt in Egypt for a period, and afterwards entered or re-entered Canaan, there is hardly a dissentient voice. The fact that Egyptian records contain no reference to the sojourn does not in the least affect the problem, for in the first place our Egyptian records are far from complete, in the second the sojourn may well have been on so small a scale that the Egyptians never thought it worthy of recording, and in the third place the Delta, which was the scene of the events, is still almost a closed book to us in early times, at least nine-tenths of our records coming from and referring to Upper Egypt.

From the Hebrew point of view a strong confirmation of the historicity of the sojourn is to be found in the fact that a period of slavery in a foreign country is not an event of which any people would be particularly proud ; and it is the very last type of incident which they would have troubled to invent. It is rather one which even if it had ever happened would tend to drop out of their traditions. That it did not do so is due to the remarkable fact that they closely connected it with the most important event in their religious experience, God's revelation of himself to them under the name of Yahweh or Jehovah (Ex. 6.3), and the establishment of a covenant between him and his people (Ex. 6.7). Now this revelation is made through Moses, who is not only the leader of the Israelites in the exodus, but is, in the story of the cradle and Pharaoh's daughter, represented as an Egyptian by upbringing. It will be clear that, whether we regard Moses as a historical figure or not, Yahweh's covenant, obviously an event of immense importance in later Hebrew eyes, is definitely connected with Egypt and the sojourn. Quite apart from all other considerations this fact makes it highly probable that the story of the sojourn in Egypt and the exodus corresponds to a definite historical fact. The precise nature of that fact and the amount of truth which is contained in the elaborate detail with which it is clothed by the narrative will be discussed in Chapters IV and V.

The third type of material, the historical, is

illustrated by the narratives of the judges, and still more by those of the kings and the later periods of history. Here the compilers had before them documents contemporary in many cases with the events which they were relating. No doubt there is still much inaccuracy of detail, the chronology given is of very dubious value, and sense of proportion is still lacking. But at the same time the main lines are historical, and agree with contemporary records from Egypt and Babylonia.

While modern scholarship has tended to restore some measure of belief in the ultimate historical basis of much of tradition, it has by no means done the same for its chronology. Tradition is always at its most untrustworthy when it comes to deal with dates and lengths of time, so much so that the wise will attribute no value whatsoever to a traditional date unless it can be shown on external grounds to be probable. The reason for this is a simple one. Oral tradition as such scarcely deals with dates at all; its formula with regard to dating is the " once upon a time " of our fairy stories. All we are entitled to expect from tradition—and even that we by no means always get—is the recognition that one event or series of events took place before, during the course of, or after another. This phenomenon is familiar to all who have lived among the less educated natives of the Near or Far East. An Egyptian peasant has no conception of his own age, or of that of any of his friends. If asked how old he is he can only reply " About as old as so-and-so," and if pressed will give figures as far apart as " Perhaps 30, perhaps 50." In other words, oral tradition preserves no absolute, but only a relative chronology.

How then are we to account for the figures which we find in the biblical narrative ? Figures appear in tradition only when some mind with a historical sense sets itself to edit tradition and to fit it into a chronological scheme. The actual material which such a mind has to draw on for time-data is naturally very small. It consists mainly in the family relations between the various personalities of the narratives, which enable time to be measured by generations. The defects of such a system are obviously many, but the worst of all is the variation observed in the number of years allotted to a generation, and the tendency to put this number higher and higher according as the tradition becomes more and more remote. Further complications arise out of the nature of the numeral systems of the nations concerned. In Babylonian legend, for instance, there is a distinct tendency to work out chronology in terms of periods of 60 years or even 3600 (60 multiplied by 60) years, 60 being a unit of the Sumerian system of numeration. Similarly in Hebrew tradition we find that a period of 40 years is constantly used, either alone or in multiples, in estimating time, 40 being a number in high favour among the Hebrews, and 40 years being perhaps regarded as a generation.

However small may be the value of the figures which appear in tradition they have to be still further discounted by the fact that even when they get into writing they are not proof against alteration. It is an axiom in palaeography that numbers are much more liable to alteration or corruption than words. There could be no more admirable example of this than the case of the Egyptian historian Manetho, who wrote about 250 B.C. a history of Egypt, which is now lost, but excerpts from which have been preserved by the later writers Eusebius, Africanus and Syncellus. Both Eusebius and Africanus give us some of Manetho's king-lists, with the names of the rulers and the lengths of their reigns, and the astonishing variations between their figures are an eloquent testimony to what may happen to numbers in a few centuries through textual corruption. If these things are possible in so short a space, what may not be possible in the case of our Bible manuscripts. Though the Pentateuch in its present form, or nearly so, had already been committed to writing as early as the fourth century B.C., yet the earliest copy which has survived dates from the tenth century A.D. It is true that we have a Greek translation of the third century B.C., and a Samaritan transcript of perhaps about the same date, but these serve only to emphasise the risk of error, for one of the most important chronological indications given by the Hebrew, namely the 430 years of the sojourn (Ex. 12.40-41) is in the Greek and in the Samaritan reduced to 215 years by the addition of the words " and in the land of Canaan " (see below, p. 27).

For these reasons we shall do well to found no very serious arguments on the chronological data offered either explicitly or implicitly by the biblical narrative, especially for the earlier periods, and there is the more need for caution since such as are to be found are almost entirely derived not from sources J and E, but from the much later P. This document has, indeed, running through it, a systematic chronology, conveyed in the form of

genealogies, from the creation to the flood
(Gen. 5 and 7.11) and from the flood to the call of
Abraham (Gen. 11.10-26 and 12.4). The Hebrew,
the Samaritan, and the Greek version differ considerably in the figures given for the various
generations—an admirable instance of the textual
corruption of numbers referred to above—and the
totals from the creation to the call of Abraham
are 2021 years in the Hebrew, 2322 in the
Samaritan, and 3407 in the Greek. The same
document P gives the period of the patriarchs'
sojourn in Canaan, from the call of Abraham to
Jacob's descent into Egypt, as 215 years. It
further, in Ex. 12.40-41, gives the length of the
sojourn in Egypt as 430 years, though even here
the Samaritan and Greek versions take this period
as including the sojourn of the patriarchs in
Canaan, thus reducing the sojourn in Egypt
to 215 years, and opening our eyes to the possibility
that the original figure of P for the sojourn may
have been 215, arrived at simply by balancing the
sojourn in Canaan with that in Egypt. In any
case, even if P originally wrote 430, the fact of its
being double 215 is suspicious, and with regard
to P's figures for the patriarchs in general it
is hardly necessary to point out that their
being based on the assumption of men living

to such ages as 175 or 180 deprives them of all value.

In Gen. 15.13 the length of the sojourn is stated to have been 400 years, a figure highly suspect, firstly as being a round number, and secondly as being ten times the stereotyped period of 40 years ; it need not, however, disagree with the 430 of Ex. 12.40-41, if we suppose the 30 years to refer to the first part of the sojourn, before oppression began.

Finally, in I Kings 6.1, we read that from the building of the temple in the fourth year of Solomon to the exodus was 480 years. Here again is a figure open to the utmost suspicion, consisting as it does in twelve periods of 40 years. It will be seen in Chapter III that the figures above mentioned give us a means of dating the descent of Jacob into Egypt, and that the date arrived at is one which would accord remarkably with the one piece of external evidence we have, namely, the known date of Amraphel or Khammurabi of Babylon. That this is the case we take to be a mere coincidence, and the fact does not in any way demonstrate the value of the figures given, the artificial nature of which is obvious at every point.

Such are in general the results of the application

to the biblical narrative of the principles of the modern sciences, more particularly of mythology and archaeology. Side by side with this external criticism went an internal criticism, mainly philological. It was observed that of certain incidents, notably the creation and flood, there were two separate accounts, differing considerably in detail. Closer examination revealed the fact that the Hebrew originals of the separate accounts showed marked differences of style, and could not possibly be due to a single writer. In other words, it was clear that the compiler of Genesis as we have it had before him two or more versions of tradition, and after the naive manner of early chroniclers he either set down both side by side, ignoring their incompatibility, or made selections from both and wove them into a single account. These various early versions used by the compiler are distinguished one from another not only by unmistakable peculiarities of style, but also by the fact that each was clearly written with some definite purpose in view. It is thus easy to break up most of the Pentateuch into the various documents from which it was compiled, and also to ascertain the rough date of the original composition of these documents.

This process is still doubtless viewed with the

utmost suspicion by many lovers of the Old Testament who wrongly associate it with atheistical propaganda, and who, reasonably perhaps, mistrust a process in which they see a critic assigning half a verse to Source E and the other half to Source J, or two critics assigning one and the same verse to different sources. But have these people followed the developments of modern philology, and do they realize that the critics who so freely cut up the Old Testament into its component parts are men whose whole lives are devoted to the study of such problems, and whose knowledge of Hebrew and of the Semitic languages in general is so great that differences of style in the Hebrew are as patent to them as they would be in the English to a layman? Suppose some portion of English History compiled from lost works by Macaulay, Gibbon and Grote, and suppose that neither the names nor any other works of these men had survived. What thoughtful reader of English could fail to be alive to the fact that there were three writers, three styles, and three different conceptions of history represented in the medley? Or imagine a history of Greece culled from works by a Herodotus, a Thucydides and a Xenophon. What intelligent sixth-form boy would fail to perceive the patchwork?

These may be exaggerated examples, but they illustrate fairly in kind if not perhaps in degree the appearance which the early books of the Old Testament present to the eyes of the Semitic philologist. He may often be in doubt as to the source of a particular sentence—there are sentences in Macaulay which Gibbon might have written and *vice versa*—he may sometimes be dogmatic when he would be wiser to confess his uncertainty, but no reasonable being can doubt that his main conclusions are right.

These conclusions may be briefly stated as follows. The chief documents from which the first five books of the Old Testament were compiled are three in number. The two oldest of these are known as J and E respectively, J having been composed in Judah during the ninth century B.C. and E in the Northern Kingdom during the eighth century B.C. The separation of J and E is not always easy, but among the most obvious differences of style may be noted the fact that E almost always uses Elohim for God, whereas J prefers Jehovah (Yahweh), and that E calls the sacred mountain Horeb, while J calls it Sinai. In general character the two documents have considerable similarity, both showing a brightness of style which is absent in the third document P ; J, however, is superior to E in literary power and in the portrayal of life and character.

Document P was written at some period during the Babylonian exile and the century which followed ; it is clearly distinguishable from both J and E in style and purpose. It comes from a priestly school and is interested in history mainly in so far as it bears on the origin of the various ceremonials of the Jewish religion.

The probable history of the compilation is as follows. During the seventh century an editor combined J and E with unimportant additions of his own. A later editor combined with this whole the discourses of Deuteronomy, and finally, in the fifth or fourth century B.C., a still later compiler combined the result with P, using P as the framework of his narrative, and giving the Pentateuch, if we disregard slight later additions, its present form.

In other words our present Pentateuch was compiled not earlier than the fifth century B.C. and contains no material written down earlier than the ninth century, except possibly certain laws and a few fragments such as the Song of Deborah. It follows at once from this that practically the whole contents of these books, as we have them, were written down only long after the time at which they were enacted.

One other point must be considered in assessing the value of our material. The early books took their present form not later than the fourth century B.C. Yet our earliest Hebrew manuscript of the Old Testament dates from the tenth century A.D. In other words we have no copy of the text until fifteen hundred years subsequent to the date of its composition. Those who are acquainted with the classics will realize what this implies, and will imagine what corruptions and alterations may take place in a text in the course of a millennium and a half. In the case of Greek and Latin authors we have some check on this, for there are generally several manuscripts, and where one is corrupt another often preserves the right reading, or, at the worst, a reading which will indicate the nature of the corruption. In the case of the Old Testament we are deprived of such an aid as this, for our manuscripts are clearly from a single source and do not contain more than about twenty variant readings in all. On the other hand we have one means of ascertaining the state of the Hebrew text as far back as the third century B.C., for it was in this century that one of the early Ptolemies

c

—possibly, but by no means certainly, Ptolemy II —of Egypt, ordered a Greek translation of the Old Testament to be made from the Hebrew text. This text was then not more than a few centuries old, and this translation, known as the Septuagint, should reproduce it almost in its original form.[1] A comparison of the two shows that on the whole the text of the Hebrew has not suffered very badly between the third century B.C. and the tenth A.D., and in some of those cases where the divergence is greatest it is to be attributed not to the fact that the old Hebrew text differed from that which has come down to us, but to the fact that the Greek translators, instead of translating quite literally the Hebrew words, substituted some sophisticated interpretation of their own. Information of a similar though less valuable nature as to the ancient Hebrew text is afforded by the Samaritan transcript made some time after 333 B.C., the Syriac, made not later than the fourth century A.D., the various Coptic translations made in the fourth to sixth centuries A.D., and the Latin Vulgate, about 400 A.D. ; but it must always be remembered that we have not the original texts of any of these versions but only

[1] The few biblical fragments found in Egypt are hardly sufficient to prove anything definite as to the state of the Hebrew text in the early centuries A.D.

much later copies which must themselves contain errors.

So much then for the nature of the material with which we have to work. For the relations of Egypt and Israel the possible corruption of the Hebrew text is fortunately not a matter of very great importance, though in one or two cases it becomes of moment. The recognition of the composite nature of the Pentateuch and of the comparatively late date of the composition even of its earliest documents is, however, vital to our subject, for it follows immediately that much of the contents of these books rests on oral tradition, and that, in consequence, all the canons which must be followed in examining and dissecting such tradition are to be observed in this case.

There is nothing unique about the early traditions of the Hebrews except the fact that they have come down to us in so complete a form. Every nation has its body of tradition. We ourselves have our Arthurian legend, Teutonic Europe has its Niebelungenlied, Egyptian literature teems with legend and tradition, and when Mesopotamia comes to be fully excavated we shall have from there a body of tradition which, for quantity, will doubtless put into the shade the contents of the Hexateuch. To set this last apart, and to refuse to apply to it the principles which are day by day making the others more intelligible and more valuable is simply intellectual dishonesty.

CHAPTER II

THE earliest tombs found in Egypt belong to a period which we are accustomed to call the Predynastic Period, because it is earlier than the Ist Dynasty, *i.e.* the first House or Line of Kings of which the Egyptians themselves have preserved any record as such. In this distant period Egypt seems to have consisted of two separate kingdoms,[1] Upper and Lower Egypt, the latter including little more than the Delta, the former the higher portions of the Nile, at least as far as El Kab. At the beginning of the Ist Dynasty a king whom later legend named Menes, but of whom we have no certain contemporary record, united the "Two Lands," as the Egyptians themselves called them, into one kingdom. Egypt continued to be a single realm until the end of the VIth Dynasty, when the country seems to have fallen into a state of anarchy. The next four dynasties, VIIth to Xth, known as the Earlier Intermediate Period, are dark to us, though light is already

---

[1] The new fragments of the Palermo Stone show, however, that there were kings of United Egypt before the Ist Dynasty.

beginning to appear. Thus in 1913 there were published for the first time two hieratic papyri in the Hermitage in Petrograd from which it becomes quite clear that these dynasties were marked by an invasion of the Egyptian Delta by Asiatics (Aamu) from the east. One of the two papyri actually describes the state of things in the Eastern Delta during the presence of the foreigners. The story, though really written after the events it describes, purports to be a prophecy written before them, and foretells a saviour for Egypt: "A king shall come from the south whose name is Ameny. . . . The Asiatics shall fall by his sword. . . . There shall be built the Wall of the Prince to prevent the Asiatics from going down into Egypt." Fortunately we can identify this saviour, for the Wall of the Prince is said, in the story of Sinuhe, to have been built by Amenemhet I, the first king of the XIIth Dynasty, to keep off the Asiatics, and Ameny is known to be nothing more than a nickname for Amenemhet, who did indeed come from a city in the south, namely Thebes. The papyrus thus has a real historical background. The other Petrograd papyrus shows us a king of the IXth or Xth Dynasty, whose name is lost, giving advice to his son Merykere, a known ruler of one of those two dynasties, which ruled at Herakleopolis. The king here describes the character of the Asiatics and relates their defeat at his own hands. " I caused the North-land to smite them ; I carried away captive their inhabitants, I plundered their cattle." He also gives his son some directions for the effective fortification of the north-eastern frontier of the Delta.

From these and from other less definite indications it may be regarded as certain that in this period between the VIth and XIth Dynasties, known to Egyptologists as the Earlier Inter-mediate Period, the Egyptian Delta was invaded by Asiatics, just as it was again in the Later Intermediate Period. This fact is of importance to us in our present quest, for it may be that we shall have to place in this interval the descent of Abram into Egypt.

The foreigners finally expelled by Amenemhet I of the XIIth Dynasty, Egypt enjoyed a period of peace and prosperity for 200 years under his able successors. It is not impossible that measures of retaliation against the Asiatics were carried out in the form of expeditions into Southern Palestine. The gravestone of a certain Sebek-khu who lived in this dynasty relates how " his majesty went down the Nile (from Thebes, the capital) to overthrow the Mentu of Sethet (Syria-Palestine). His majesty arrived at a region whose name is Sekmem." Here a fight took place with the Asiatics, in which Sebek-khu distinguished himself by taking a prisoner. Max Müller has attempted to identify Sekmem with Shechem, but the philological difficulties in the way of this identification are very great, and it is more probable that Sekmem is some place in Southern Palestine, or even nearer to the Egyptian frontier than this. There are other indications of warfare with Nearer Asia during this dynasty, but they do not enable us to form any clear idea of the operations, or even to assert that a definite career of conquest in that country was embarked upon by the Egyptian kings.

At the end of the XIIth Dynasty Egypt once more became a prey to internal confusion. Once more she paid the penalty of her position in a fertile valley at the western end of the isthmus which led into Africa from the over-populated Nearer Asia ; once more the Delta was invaded by Asiatics. The details of this invasion are again obscure, and so little do we know of the XIIIth to XVIIth Dynasties that we can find for them no better name than the Later Intermediate

Period. The period was one on which the Egyptians of later days looked back with loathing and hatred, together with a keen desire to forget, which is doubtless in part responsible for our ignorance of what actually happened.

Before we can bring these Asiatic invasions of Egypt into any relation with the biblical story we must decide to what dates they are to be assigned. Here there is a serious preliminary difficulty. The student of history who finds two Egyptological authorities assigning dates 2,000 years apart to one and the same event is liable to be dismayed and discouraged, and it is therefore necessary to explain how this vast discrepancy arises.

There are two methods by which Egyptian dating may be established; firstly by adding together the lengths of single reigns or dynasties as given in the history written in Greek about 250 B.C. by the Egyptian priest Manetho, and now lost, save for excerpts preserved by later historians, and secondly by the astronomical method. This last is based on the fact that the Egyptian civil year consisted of only 365 days (12 months of 30 days each, and 5 "additional days") instead of about $365\frac{1}{4}$; in other words the Egyptians had no Leap Year. Owing to this the civil year kept getting out of gear with the true or solar year, and consequently with the seasons, the error obviously amounting to a quarter of a day each year, or a day in four years, a month in 120 years, and so on, until after 1460 years (365 multiplied by 4) the beginning of the civil and solar years coincided once more. The Egyptians were not unacquainted with this shift of the calendar, for they measured the true or solar year by observing the heliacal rising[1] of the star Sothis or Sirius. The consequence is that whenever we find it stated in a text or inscription dated to a certain year of a certain king that Sothis in that year rose heliacally on a certain date of the civil year, we can ascertain the amount of the divergence between civil and solar years at that date.

Now we learn from the Roman writer Censorinus that the beginning of the civil year coincided with that of the solar or Sothic year in 139 A.D., and from what has been said above it will easily be seen that the same thing would have happened 1,460 years previously, *i.e.* in 1321 B.C., and again 1,460 years before that, *i.e.* in 2781 B.C., and so on. These periods of 1,460

[1] A star is said to rise heliacally when it first appears again above the eastern horizon at sunrise after having been for some time invisible in that position.

years from 139 A.D. to 1321 B.C., from 1321 B.C.
to 2781 B.C., etc., are called Sothic Periods.

Returning now to our ascertained shift of the
civil year, it is clear that this will enable us to
fix a certain year of a certain king to its correct
position in a Sothic Period, but, and here comes
the rub, it will not tell us which Sothic Period.
Thus, when we find in the Ebers Medical Papyrus
a calendar informing us that, in the ninth year
of King Amenhotp I of the XVIIIth Dynasty,
Sothis rose heliacally on the ninth day of the
eleventh month of the civil year, we can see that
at this moment the shift had made a full cycle
all but 57 days, made up of the 22 remaining
days (including the ninth) of the eleventh month,
30 of the twelfth and the five " additional days "
added on by the Egyptians to their twelve months
of thirty days each to complete the 365. The
year in question was therefore 228 years before
the completion of a Sothic Cycle. Now in this
case we happen to know from comparisons with
Mesopotamian and other history that the cycle
in question can have been no other than that
which ended in 1321 B.C. Adding to this the
228 years we get 1549 for the year in question.[1]

[1] Strictly speaking, since Sirius rose on the same day of the civil
calendar four years in succession, any of the years 1550-1547 B.C. would
suit.

So far so good. All Egyptologists are agreed on this dating, which brings the beginning of the XVIIIth Dynasty to roughly 1580 B.C. The trouble begins when we go back to the XIIth Dynasty and find that in the seventh year of Senusret III Sothis rose on the 16th day of the eighth civil month. Reckoning as before, we can show that this year must have fallen 560 years before the end of a Sothic Cycle. But which Sothic Cycle, that which ended in 2781 B.C., or that which ended in 1321 B.C. ? Here we have no obvious comparisons to guide us. Most Egyptologists, especially those of Germany and America, vote for the second and thereby get about 1882 B.C.[1] for the year in question, and roughly 2000 B.C. for the beginning of the XIIth Dynasty. A few, with Petrie in their van, are convinced that the earlier cycle is the right one, and thus get a date of about 3460 B.C., a whole Sothic Cycle earlier, for the beginning of the XIIth Dynasty.

The discrepancy which amazes the layman is now explained. We must either choose between these two dates, or suppose that some flaw exists in the Sothic method of reckoning, which is, it must be confessed, not very probable.

---

[1] Strictly speaking, since Sirius rose on the same day of the civil calendar four years in succession, any of the years 1882-1879 B.C. would suit.

It should be noted that the Long Dating is at first sight far more in accordance than the Short with the addition of lengths of reigns as given by Manetho and in part supported by the Turin Papyrus of Kings. This fact, as may well be imagined, is made the most of by the supporters, not very numerous, of the Long Dating, but it is rightly pointed out by their opponents that many of the kings and even some of the dynasties given by Manetho in the obscure Intermediate Periods probably reigned simultaneously in different parts of Egypt. King's astonishing discovery that the IInd Babylonian Dynasty ruled not in Babylon itself but in the Country of the Sea, and may therefore for chronological purposes be eliminated from the king-lists, has shortened dates in Mesopotamia by centuries, thereby not only warning us not to overdate the parallel periods in Egypt, but illustrating the danger of dating by the mere addition of reign-lengths in king-lists.

Many of us, too, in view of the archaeological evidence, find it impossible to believe that the Later Intermediate Period lasted nearly 1,700 years, as it must have done on the Long Dating theory. So few are the remains which this period has left in Egypt, and so inconsiderable the development in art and civilisation between the XIIth Dynasty and the XVIIIth that the 200 years postulated by the Short Dating seem not insufficient. The recent publication of a cylinder of lapis lazuli, inscribed partly in Babylonian cuneiform of a style which can hardly be much earlier than 2000 B.C. and partly in Egyptian with the cartouche of Amenemhet I, the first king of the XIIth Dynasty, will prove a hard nut to crack for those who would date this dynasty to something like 3500 B.C. For these and other reasons too complex to be discussed here the shorter chronology, which places the beginning of the XIIth Dynasty at about 2000 B.C., has been adopted in this volume.

Behind the XIIth Dynasty all is guesswork, for no Sothic datings have been preserved. Since the dates of the earlier Egyptian periods are of little importance for our present purpose suffice it to state that the advocates of the Short Dating imagine the 1st Dynasty to have begun about 3300 B.C., while the other school of thought speaks of dates ranging from 4000 to 5000 B.C. for this event.

CHAPTER III

ABRAM'S DESCENT INTO EGYPT

"And Abram went down into Egypt to sojourn there; for the famine was grievous in the land."

In these words we find our first biblical point of contact between the history of Egypt and that of the Israelites. Abram has just left Haran and journeyed through the land of the Canaanites, passing Bethel "going on still toward the south." It is at this point that famine forces him to descend into Egypt.

Before going any further with this story one possibility must be considered, the possibility that it is nothing more than a "duplication"[1] of the descent of Jacob into Egypt. It is often difficult and even impossible to prove, or even to establish a probability, that any particular incident in a tradition is a duplication, and in the case before us the data are so slight that

[1] Duplication is the invention of two separate legends to cover a single set of facts, or the attribution by tradition of a single set of exploits to two different persons or groups of persons. Thus, in the present case the question to be asked is, whether a single descent of certain persons or tribes into Egypt may not have given rise to two separate traditions, the one connected with the name of Abram and the other with that of Jacob.

we can make no progress. Two details alone
are common to both stories, firstly, the ascrip-
tion of both descents into Egypt to famine,
and secondly, the fact that in both cases
Pharaoh sends the Hebrews out of his land in
consequence of plagues. The first point is of
little significance, for the most natural reason for
tradition to give for any descent into Egypt
would be " a famine in the land." In the case
of the second point of similarity the resemblance
is by no means a close one in detail.

It cannot then be satisfactorily shown that the
descent of Abram is a mere doubling of that of
Jacob, and it may quite well be that it contains
an actual kernel of fact. Can we, from Egyptian
history, get any conception of what this consisted in ?

In the last chapter we have referred to those
two great overflowings of Asiatic peoples from
Nearer Asia into the Delta of the Nile which
took place in the Earlier and Later Intermediate
Periods respectively, that is to say, the one
shortly before 2000 B.C. and the other between
1780 and 1580 B.C. Is the descent of Abram, be
he a man or be he a tribe, into Egypt a distant
echo of one of these movements, and if so, of
which of the two ?

A fortunate accident of tradition enables us to decide between the two. In Genesis 14.1 we are told that " Amraphel king of Shinar, Arioch king of Ellasar, Chedorlaomer king of Elam, and Tidal king of nations " made war with certain of the peoples of Canaan who had been subject to them for thirteen years and rebelled in the fourteenth. Now the names of these kings are not mere inventions of the historian. However much they may have suffered in transmission, they are the names of actual historical kings, and the great battle of five kings with four probably corresponds to a historical fact.

Search has been made on the Mesopotamian side for kings with which these four could reasonably be identified. It is not possible here to enter into the controversy which has raged round the various identifications proposed, and we must content ourselves by giving the main results. In the first place there is a fairly general agreement that in Amraphel of Shinar we may recognize Khammurabi of the Ist Dynasty of Babylon. The reader who is unacquainted with the subject of Semitic phonetics may stand aghast at the proposal to equate two names which at first sight have so little in common. Two things, however, must be pointed out : firstly, that in the trans-

D

mission of names in Semitic the vowels have little importance, for in most Semitic dialects they were not written and hence peculiarly liable to be altered in handing on ; and secondly it must be noted that in Khammurabi and Amraphel we have three consonants alike, namely m, r and b, the last weakened in the Hebrew to ph (*i.e.* f). The absence in the Hebrew form of the initial Kh is a little disconcerting, though the form Ammurabi does occur once in a Babylonian document of the king's own reign. The final -el in the Hebrew is perhaps less disturbing, and several not unreasonable explanations of it have been given. On the whole it may be said that the identification is distinctly probable. Arioch of Ellasar has by some been equated with Eriaku, a dialectal Sumerian form of the name of Warad Sin, king of Larsa, a town in Sumeria or South Babylonia (Map 1). Up till quite recently this seemed a not unreasonable proposition, but unfortunately the discovery of the famous date-list of the Dynasty of Larsa puts it out of court. It had long been known that Kudur-mabuk, father of Warad Sin, and king of Elam, a district in the west of Persia, conquered Larsa from the Sumerians and placed his son on the throne. It therefore seemed not at all unreasonable to find

Warad Sin (Eriaku) in league with a king of Elam,
Chedorlaomer, against the cities of Canaan, he
being himself an Elamite. The difficulty raised
by the Larsa date-list is that it proves
Khammurabi, another member of the league, to
have come to the throne no less than thirty years
after the death of Warad Sin. The suggestion
that the Jewish historian mentioned Warad Sin
in mistake for his successor on the throne of Larsa,
Rim Sin, is not worthy of consideration, for what
we are concerned with is not what he might have
said but what he actually did say. It is far wiser
to suppose that Eriaku and Arioch are not one
and the same, especially as it is far from certain
that Ellasar is Larsa, there being considerable
difficulty in deriving the one from the other
without doing violence to phonetic laws.

With regard to Chedorlaomer, we know as yet
of no king of Elam bearing this name, but it has
been pointed out that the name may well be the
Hebrew form of Kudur-lagamar, the element
Kudur being frequent in Elamite names of this
period (*e.g.* Kudur-mabuk), and Lagamar
occurring in an Assyrian text as the name of an
Elamite deity. Tidal, king of nations or Goiim,
is unknown, but Sayce has pointed out that the
name is probably Hittite.

Even supposing that we could accept all these identifications there would still be difficulties in our way, for the account in Gen. 14 represents these four rulers as allies in a campaign against the dynasts of Eastern Palestine. Yet from archaeological and inscriptional evidence in Mesopotamia it is clear that Khammurabi was throughout the deadly foe of Elam and of the Elamite dynasty in Larsa, rather than their ally. But surely this need not be pressed, and we need hardly expect to find the Jewish chronicler quite *au fait* with the complicated state of politics in Babylonia and Persia. Let it suffice that he has preserved for us some record, valuable if hazy, of hostile contact between the peoples of Palestine and those of the east, dating, if our identification of Amraphel be correct, as far back as the reign of Khammurabi. Now until the time of King's discovery that the Ist and IInd Dynasties of Babylon partly overlapped, and that the IInd ruled not at Babylon but in the Country of the Sea, many Assyriologists placed the reign of Khammurabi as far back as 2400 B.C. The new discovery naturally shortened the dates considerably, and a fresh piece of evidence of an entirely different type has fixed the reign with some certainty. The Dutch astronomer Kugler has worked out certain observations of the heliacal rising and setting of the planet Venus taken in the reign of King Ammi-zaduga of the Ist Babylonian Dynasty, and recorded on a cuneiform tablet, and has found to what years these must refer. The result of his work is to fix the accession of Ammi-zaduga to 1977 B.C., and consequently that of Khammurabi to 2123 B.C.

Now, if Khammurabi is the Amraphel of Genesis who fought in the battle of the four kings against five, in which Lot was made captive and afterwards released by Abram, it is clear that Abram had returned from Egypt before the death of Khammurabi in 2081 B.C. This date is satisfactory from the Egyptian point of view, for if Abram left Egypt not later than 2081 B.C., his sojourn must have fallen into the period just preceding the XIIth Dynasty, which, it will be remembered, was in Egypt a time of anarchy and Asiatic invasion. From recent discoveries we know that though Amenemhet I, the Ameny of the Petrograd papyrus, was regarded as the saviour of Egypt, and was the builder of the great wall in the Eastern Delta made to keep back the Asiatics, yet the war of liberation had already begun under his predecessors of the XIth Dynasty, the Antefs and Mentuhotps of Thebes, and the retirement of Abram may conceivably have been due to pressure by the Egyptian armies.

It is a curious coincidence that the date obtained from the Babylonian evidence for Abram's return from Egypt corresponds almost exactly with that given by the Hebrew chronology. In I Kings 6.1 we are told that from the foundation of Solomon's temple back to the exodus was 480 years. The foundation of the temple can be fairly accurately fixed by reckoning back from the known Assyrian date, 854 B.C., for the battle of Qarqar, at which Ahab and Benhadad II (Hadad-idri) of Damascus were allies. There is considerable reason for placing this alliance (I Kings 20.34) in Ahab's twenty-first year, and reckoning back by the lengths of reigns as given in I Kings we get 970 for the accession of Solomon and therefore 966 for the beginning of the Temple in his fourth year (I Kings 6.1). The traditional date for the exodus was thus about 1446 B.C. In Ex. 12.40 the length of the sojourn in Egypt is said to be 430 years, a number with which the 400 years given in Gen. 15.15 for the length of the oppression need not disagree. The descent of Jacob into Egypt would thus fall about 1876 B.C. Now Jacob was 130 years old when he went into Egypt, and was therefore

born about 2006 B.C. Isaac, who was 60 when
Jacob was born, must have been born in 2066 B.C.,
and since his birth took place after the return of
his father from Egypt to Canaan this last must
have happened before, perhaps very shortly
before, 2066 B.C.

According to the Hebrews' own tradition then
this is the date to which the Egyptian incident is
to be attributed, and it will be seen that this date
differs by only fifteen years from that obtained
from the Babylonian evidence. After what has
been said in Chapter I concerning the chronology
of the Hebrew compilers it is hardly necessary to
point out that this coincidence is purely fortuitous
and has no corroborative value whatsoever.

We may sum up the results of this investigation
as follows. If the descent of Abram into Egypt is
not a mere " double " of a later incident, and if
Hebrew tradition is correct in making Abram,
whether this be the name of a historical individual
or stand merely for a particular people or tribe,
the contemporary of Amraphel of Babylon, then
Abram must have left Egypt before 2081 B.C.
In this case the descent into Egypt must have
fallen into the Earlier Intermediate Period, and
it is not impossible that the story is the echo in
Hebrew tradition of that Asiatic invasion of

Egypt to which the Petrograd papyri (p. 38-39) bear unwilling testimony on the Egyptian side.

We are now able to place the movements of Abram and his tribe in their correct position in the early history of the Middle East. It is believed by many geographers that the land of Arabia is subject to periodic droughts, which, recurring in long cycles of centuries, drive the pastoral peoples of the land out into the neighbouring countries in search of pastures for their flocks. History records four main eruptions of these Semites or primitive Arabians (Map 1). The first gave the Semitic dynasty of Sargon and Naram-sin to Akkadia or Northern Babylonia, and took place before 2500 B.C. The second, which happened about five hundred years later, gave to Canaan its Semitic people and to Babylon its Ist Dynasty. The third, shortly after 1500 B.C., is represented by the Aramaeans, and the fourth is the great Moorish movement of the seventh century A.D.

It is to the second of these eruptions that the episode of Abram is to be assigned. The memories of this great movement must have survived long in Hebrew tradition, and are undoubtedly reflected in the accounts of the original coming of Abram's

family or tribe from Ur of the Chaldees and from
Haran. It is hardly worth while to point out
that, supposing the Hebrews to have come from
Ur in South Babylonia, Haran on the Middle
Euphrates would have lain directly on their
shortest, indeed their only route into Canaan (Map
1), for it is quite probable that in the names Ur and
Haran two entirely separate traditions survive as
to the early home of the Hebrews, and there is
little point in an attempt to combine them.
The names may in this case have no historical
value whatsoever, and merely indicate a later
belief in an eastern origin. So far as we can see at
present the second Semitic movement, to which
we are inclined to attribute the migration of
Abram, apparently took a course precisely opposed
to that indicated by the itinerary Ur-Haran-
Canaan. The Semites who invaded Babylonia
and founded the Dynasty of Nisin and the
Ist Dynasty of Babylon were apparently Western
Semites, who, having perhaps moved up from
Arabia into Canaan, proceeded to conquer Syria,
the Middle Euphrates, and finally Babylonia.
The recent excavations at Ur have discovered no
traces whatsoever of any early Semitic occupation
such as the Hebrew tradition would suggest, the
early remains found being either partly, as would

be expected in this region, Sumerian, and partly, according to one of the excavators, even pre-Sumerian. On the other hand it is necessary to remember that the site is by no means fully excavated as yet.

It is a curious fact that both Ur and Haran were in early times centres of moon-worship. This can hardly be a coincidence, and the guess may be hazarded that their appearance side by side as places of Hebrew origin may be due to the fact that they were introduced to explain the prevalence of moon-worship at some stage in the life history of one or more Hebrew tribes. There is, of course, no direct trace of this in the Bible narrative, unless we accept the dubious derivation of the sacred mountain Sinai from the Babylonian moon-god Sin, but it is a very usual process in the accumulation of tradition. It has, however, been pointed out that a god called Ya-u was known in Babylonia at the time of the Ist Dynasty, and that this name is equivalent with Yeho or Yo, the shorter form of Yahweh, used in Hebrew personal names compounded with the name of the deity, such as Joab, Jehoshaphat. This fact, together with the probable Babylonian origin of the name Abram and its variant Abraham, tends to confirm the connection of Abram with the second Semitic migration, which was responsible for the Ist Dynasty of Babylon. It is further worthy of remark that the names Sarah and Milcah, the patriarch's wife and sister-in-law, are identical with Sharratu[1] and Malkatu[1], two members, side by side with Sin, of the pantheon of Haran. Some authorities would go further still and attempt to show the identity of the Hebrew Yahweh with the Babylonian Moon-god, and their evidence, even if not conclusive, is not to be lightly set aside.

Leaving aside doubtful questions, it may be said that the evidence justifies the conclusion that the story of the migrations of Abram preserves some faint record of the second great Semitic migration. The direct connection of the Hebrew ancestors with Ur and Haran we may either accept as literally true, or explain as a later conception invented to account for the known lunar nature of certain elements in Hebrew religion.

Does the colouring of the narrative of Abram's stay in Egypt help us in determining either its authenticity or its date ? Unfortunately it is too vague and too scanty to afford any real help. The undignified incident of Abram's passing his

---

[1] The -atu is the feminine ending in Assyrian just as -ah is in Hebrew.

wife off as his sister in order to save his own skin
has been cited, with a backing of mistranslations
or misconceptions from Egyptian documents, as in
peculiarly close keeping with Egyptian customs.
With regard to Abram's camels, often quoted as
Egyptian local colour, it should be pointed out
that the camel was not introduced into Egypt
until centuries after this period ; the Ist Dynasty
skeletons of " camels " which have found their way
into several books proving on examination to be
those of donkeys.   On the other hand there is no
reason *a priori* why a Semite going down into
Egypt should not be accompanied by camels.

Before concluding this chapter it is impossible
to refrain from mentioning a very famous scene
from an Egyptian tomb which has appeared in
more than one book with the title " The arrival of
Abram in Egypt," and has doubtless misled many.
In the tomb of an Egyptian noble called
Khnemhotp at Beni Hasan is painted, among
other episodes of his career, a scene in which a
scribe called Neferhotp leads before him a small
group of Aamu or Syrians.   Their leader, identified by early writers with Abram, is called " Ruler
of a foreign country," and his name is given as
Ibsha.   The incriptions accompanying the scene

inform us that 37 of the Syrians or Aamu were brought bearing green eye-paint, in the sixth year of Senusret II of the XIIth Dynasty, the date of which year would be roughly 1900 B.C. Now the identification with Abram and his family, fantastic in any case, is made quite impossible by the fact that the leader's name is Ibsha. At the same time the scene is not without interest to the biblical student. Though these are not Abram and his family they are men and women and children of his race or of one akin to his, brought to Egypt with presents or tribute not many decades after Abram himself had left the country. Their spears and bows and throw-sticks are the weapons which Abram himself must have carried, and the lyre which we see in the hands of one of the group was perhaps an instrument to whose sound Jehovah was praised. The facial characteristics, totally un-Egyptian, are those of the Israelites, and in the long gaudy cloaks which some of the male figures wear we may see the counterpart of Joseph's " coat of many colours."[1]

Finally, this picture reflects the Egyptian attitude towards the native of Syria during this

[1] More accurately " a tunic of palms and soles," *i.e.* a long cloak reaching to the hands and feet.

period. In the first place it is to be noted that
the word Syrians is followed by a determinative
sign representing a captive with hands tied behind
him. It would be unwise to argue from this
that these people were captives taken in war, but
it is quite clear that the Egyptians regarded them
as a people whom they had once defeated and
driven out, and whom were they wont to defeat.
After the expulsion of the Asiatics from Egypt by
Ameny, it is probable that the Egyptians carried
the war into the enemies' country. Reference
has been made above to the gravestone of an
Egyptian officer called Sebek-khu, which mentions
a campaign in which Sebek-khu followed his
king Amenemhet III into Syria, where a battle
took place near a place called Sekmem. In the
tomb of a certain Dhouthotp, who lived about
the same time, at El Bersheh, are shown captive
Syrian cattle to whom a herdsman is saying
" Once ye trod the sand, now ye walk on herbage,"
an obvious allusion to the bleak and desert
nature which every good Egyptian attributed
to Syria as contrasted with his own fertile
homeland.

From these and similar indications, such as
the occurrence in temple documents of this
period of a type of temple-slave called simply

Aamu or Syrians, we may gather that the position of the patriarchs, or the tribes for whose history they stand, in or about South Palestine was not altogether a secure one, that region being, if not subject to Egypt, at least liable to attack by slave- and cattle-raiding expeditions. It would not surprise us if Abram, like his kinsman Ibsha, occasionally thought it wise to propitiate the King of Egypt with a gift.

CHAPTER IV

" AND they took their cattle and their goods . . . and came into Egypt, Jacob, and all his seed with him."

Nature of the sojourn and exodus.

Before entering upon any discussion concerning the date of the sojourn, and the date and route of the exodus, it is necessary to ask exactly what we mean by these two events.

It has been explained in Chapter I that tradition is often incorrect in detail, that its chronology is generally poor, that it telescopes and duplicates, and that its geography is rarely consistent. But in most cases in which archaeology has permitted a test the central facts of tradition have been found to contain some kernel of truth. Thus in the case of the sojourn we may consider it as highly probable, if not certain, that at some period in the history of the Hebrews one or more of their tribes or clans did actually visit Egypt, sojourn there, and afterwards return to Canaan. This fact became an integral part of the tradition preserved by this tribe or these tribes, from whence it passed into the general tradition of the Hebrews.

A belief in the fact of a sojourn and an exodus does not, however, involve of necessity a belief in any of the detail with which they are invested in the biblical narrative. On the contrary it will be the aim of some of the following pages to show how a very simple story became gradually encrusted with accretions of later and very various dates. What then was the real nature of the episode, and can we find any trace of it in Egyptian history ?[1]

An Egyptian papyrus known as Anastasi VI contains a letter from an Egyptian frontier official stationed at the eastern entrance of the Wadi Tumilat (see below pp. 79-80), in which we find the following words : " We have finished causing the Bedawi tribes of Edom to pass the fortress of Merenptah, belonging to Theku, towards the pools of Pithom (of) Merenptah, belonging to Theku, in order to feed themselves

---

[1] The theory of Winckler, adopted by Cheyne, to the effect that the Mizraim in which the Hebrews sojourned was not Egypt but a hypothetical land of Musri, in Arabia, has been so often and so effectively refuted as to need only a passing mention here.

E

and to feed their flocks." From this it is clear that the Egyptians of the XIXth Dynasty or later were in the habit of allowing some of the Bedawi tribes on their eastern frontier to use the district called Theku, in the Wadi Tumilat, as a pasturage (Map 2). If this custom obtained at earlier dates it is by no means impossible that certain Hebrew tribes had at some time been among those to whom this privilege was accorded, and in such a visit we might easily see the basis of the story of the sojourn and exodus. On the other hand it is thought by some that despite the low number, seventy, which the biblical tradition gives to the immigrants, the sojourn must have referred to something on a larger scale than this, to have assumed so important a place in Hebrew history, even supposing that originally it formed part of the tradition of only one tribe or group of tribes.

If this view be taken, and there is much to be said for it, some larger event in the history of Egypt must be looked for. There is no difficulty in finding such an event. We saw that the descent of Abram into Egypt, if not a mere duplication of the descent of Jacob, might not unreasonably be brought into connection with the invasion of the Egyptian Delta by Asiatic

Semites in the Earlier Intermediate Period which separates the VIth from the XIIth Dynasty. Similarly the descent of Jacob and his seed, if we are to regard it as a tribal or folk migration of any size and importance, and not the mere isolated movement of a single family, would seem to fall most naturally into the Later Intermediate Period, between the XIIth and the XVIIIth Dynasties. During the prosperous days of the XIIth Dynasty we can hardly conceive a foreign people being allowed to make their way into Egypt in any considerable force, though it should be remembered that we are in almost complete ignorance of conditions in the Delta during that period. But in the days of confusion which followed the fall of that dynasty the Delta became the prey of an Asiatic people, known to us as the Hyksos, and the temptation to bring Jacob's descent into connection with this incursion is almost irresistible.

Who then were the Hyksos and from whence did they come? The Egyptian historian Manetho begins his account of them in the following manner. "There was a king of ours whose name was Timaios, in whose reign it came to pass, I know not why, that God was displeased with us, and there came unexpectedly men of ignoble

birth out of the eastern parts, who had boldness
enough to make an expedition into our country
and easily subdued it without a battle.   And
when they had got our rulers under their power,
they afterwards savagely burned down our cities
and demolished the temples of the gods and used
all the inhabitants in a most hostile manner, for
they slew some and led the children and wives of
others into slavery.   At length they made one
of themselves king whose name was Salatis, and
he lived at Memphis and made both Upper and
Lower Egypt pay tribute, and left garrisons in
places which were most suitable for them."   The
account goes on to tell us that these people made
their capital at a place called Avaris, in the Delta.
Manetho further informs us that the word
Hyksos consists of two parts, *hyk*, which means
in Egyptian, a ruler, and *sos*, which he says
means shepherd, but, he adds, "only in the
vulgar tongue."   Now although it is true that
hyk is good Egyptian for a ruler it has sometimes
been said that there is no Egyptian word *sos*
meaning shepherd. Quite lately, however, a
German scholar has pointed out that the Egyptian
shos, a general name for the Asiatic bedawin who
lived on the fringes of the Delta between Egypt
and Palestine, came in later times to have the

meaning of shepherds, these people being mainly pastoral in their pursuits. It would therefore seem that Manetho was not erring when he translated Hyksos as Shepherd Kings.

It has also been shown quite recently that Avaris, which had previously been identified with Tell el-Yahudiyeh in the Eastern Delta, is in reality the same as the later Pelusium, at the mouth of the most easterly or Pelusiac branch of the Nile, now dried up (Map 2). This would be the obvious position for the capital of a people who were ruling not only the Egyptian Delta but also Palestine. This, added to the fact that the Egyptians, when they drove out the invaders, pursued them into Palestine and besieged them in the town of Sharuhen, places it almost beyond doubt that the invaders were a people who came from the direction of Palestine. This being so it becomes extremely probable that in the story of the descent of Jacob into Egypt Hebrew tradition has preserved the memory of some episode or group of episodes in this Asiatic invasion of Egypt.

The period was one on which the Egyptians looked back with hatred and shame, and it is with apparent unwillingness that they chronicle any events connected with it. This aversion to the invaders was religious as well as political, for the god of the conquerors was the hated Set or Sutekh, and they seem to have pursued a definite policy of destroying the temples of the Egyptian gods. Thus Queen Hatshepsut of the XVIIIth Dynasty tells us in an inscription over a sacred cave at Beni Hasan " I have re-established that which was in ruins, I have raised up that which was previously destroyed, when the Asiatics were in the midst of Avaris in the Delta, overthrowing that which had been made, while they ruled in ignorance of Ra." Here the opposition of the Hyksos to the Egyptian state worship of Ra, the sun-god, is clearly brought out.

Although the Egyptian monuments give us few details with regard to the actual rule of the Hyksos they do furnish us with some information as to the final expulsion of the intruders by the Kings of the XVIIth and early XVIIIth Dynasties. A folk-story preserved in a papyrus (Sallier I) in the British Museum records a curiously obscure interchange of messages between an Egyptian King Seqenenre, ruling at Thebes in Upper Egypt (the modern Luxor), and the Hyksos Apophis, ruling at Avaris in the Delta. The latter makes a complaint against " the pool of the hippopotamus which is in Thebes, for they permit me no sleep day or night, the noise of them is in my ear." Although the exact nature of the complaint which is expressed in these figurative words is unknown to us, it is clear that we here have the Hyksos king attempting to pick a quarrel with Seqenenre, doubtless with the intention of making it an excuse for the invasion and annexation of Upper Egypt. The damaged papyrus only allows us to conjecture that King Seqenenre attempted to extricate himself by offers of increased tribute. But the tables were soon to be turned, and a glimpse of the turning has come down to us in a romantic way. While excavating at Thebes some years ago, Lord Carnarvon discovered a wooden tablet which had served some Egyptian boy as a copy-book. On it is written in ink a copy of part of an inscription evidently set up in stone in some temple, and now lost to us. Here we find King Kames, the last king of the XVIIth Dynasty, actually engaged in the task of expelling the Hyksos. "I have gone forth victorious" he says, "to drive back the Asiatics by the command of Amon. I stopped the Asiatics, I freed Egypt. I drove him out, I hacked down his wall, I slew his people, I caused my soldiers to embark like wolves with their prey, with slaves and cattle, dividing their property." Here we have clearly the middle stages of the war of expulsion, which had doubtless been begun by Kames' predecessors, the three Seqenenres. The mummy of one of these, perhaps the one mentioned in the hippopotamus story, has actually been found at Thebes, and it is clear from its condition that the king was killed in battle at some distance from Thebes. The skull bears the mark of a heavy blow in front of the left ear ; over the right eye there is a spear wound, and the left side of the skull has been cleft by a mortal blow from a battle axe.

We should not infer from Kames' glowing account of his prowess that he put a decisive end to the Hyksos peril, for we find his successor, Aahmes, left with the task of besieging and sacking Avaris, the Hyksos capital in Egypt. This we know from the tomb-biography of a famous Egyptian admiral who bore the same name as the king himself. The Egyptian army was apparently conveyed to the Delta by river, and two actions took place near Avaris, in which our admiral distinguished himself and gained the decoration known as the " gold of valour." "We took Avaris" he proceeds, " and I carried off as captives from thence one man and three women, in all four, and his majesty gave them to me for slaves." This surely marks the final sack of Avaris and the expulsion of the Hyksos from Egypt, for the next campaign in which the admiral took part was in Southern Palestine, where the Egyptians captured Sharuhen. So ends, shortly after 1580 B.C., the history of the Hyksos in Egypt.

Such is the period into which the entry of the Hebrews into Egypt would seem most naturally to fall. It would explain very simply the fact that the newcomers at first met with good treatment at the hands of the " King of Egypt " for, from the point of view of a people dwelling in Goshen, probably a region in the Eastern Delta, the King of Egypt would be the Hyksos King reigning at Avaris, doubtless related by race to the Hebrews themselves, and not the Egyptian king reigning, probably in a half dependent state, at Thebes in Upper Egypt. Should we care to go into details it would further explain the favour with which Joseph was received by the king, and, should we care to assume that the Jacob tribes were not the first of the Asiatics to move into the Delta, the apportioning to them of the land of Goshen would be merely an incident in the allotment of the captured Egyptian Delta to the invading tribes as they arrived. If we accept this it is easy to explain the " king who knew not Joseph " as the first, or at any rate as one of the true Egyptian kings who again ruled the Delta after the expulsion of the invaders. In this case we are forced to believe that certain of the invaders had escaped expulsion and were suffered to remain in the Delta, but in a subservient position, and under conditions which became more and more severe as the Egyptians felt themselves more thoroughly masters of the Delta, and more free from the fear of any recurrence of the irruption. This solution is that which has been most generally adopted by scholars, partly, perhaps, because it avoids the rejection of the biblical chronology of 400 years for the sojourn, and partly because on no other hypothesis can the state of things prevailing during the later part of the sojourn be accepted as at all probable. At the same time it is to be noted that some scholars, and in particular Dr. H. R. Hall, are more inclined to believe that the exodus must be considered as an incident in the expulsion of the Hyksos, the supposition that any portion of this people was allowed to live on in the Delta being regarded by them as most improbable. Dr. Hall thus dates the exodus to roughly

1580 B.C., and since he holds that in the Khabiru of the Tell el-Amarna letters (about 1380 B.C.) we are to see the Hebrews under Joshua entering Palestine, he is forced to lengthen the 40 years wandering in the wilderness to 200. From the biblical point of view this involves serious chronological difficulties, and for this and other reasons the view has not been very widely accepted by scholars.

Although an attempt has been made in this chapter to show that the entry of the Jacob tribes into Egypt might reasonably have fallen into the Hyksos period, which began not earlier than 1780 and ended in about 1580 B.C., it cannot be too strongly asserted that the point is one which cannot be proved. Archaeology is not an exact science, and deals more often in probabilities and possibilities than in irrefutable demonstrations. It is therefore by no means surprising to find that some authorities do not accept a Hyksos date for the entry into Egypt. Burney, for instance, points out that the Samaritan transcript of the Bible, as well as the Greek Septuagint, which, be it remembered, is a translation from Hebrew versions many centuries older than the earliest which has survived to our days, gives 430 years for the sojourn in Egypt

" *and in the land of Canaan,*" that is to say for
the whole patriarchal period. On biblical
reckoning the period in Canaan adds up to 215
years, and thus the same period, namely 215 years,
is left for the sojourn in Egypt. Now Burney
accepts the very widely held belief, which we
shall discuss later (pp. 105 ff.) that the exodus took
place under King Merenptah of the XIXth
Dynasty, about 1225-1215 B.C., and by adding
215 years to this he obtains for the rough date
of the entry the year 1435 B.C., a year which falls
within the reign of King Amenhotp II of
the XVIIIth Dynasty, the very reign to which,
as will be seen later, some writers would assign
the exodus. From the Egyptian point of view
there is nothing intrinsically impossible about this
view. It is not impossible that a small Asiatic
tribe should have been allowed by the Egyptians
to settle in the land of Goshen in the reign of
Amenhotp II, as we know from the passage from
Papyrus Anastasi VI quoted above (p. 65).
On the other hand it should be clearly understood
that Burney's view involves throwing over the
430 years given by the Hebrew text of the Bible
for the sojourn, as well as the identification of
the Khabiru of the Tell el-Amarna letters with
the Hebrews under Joshua. He may be justified

in both cases (see below pp. 120-123). Whatever view we adopt, the Hebrew chronology offers difficulties, and the identification of Khabiru with Hebrews is not certain, though probable. However this may be, the present writer is inclined to think that a more consistent and intelligible account of the sojourn is to be had by placing the entry, as suggested earlier in this chapter, in the Hyksos period.

The geography of the sojourn.

There is nothing which lends at first sight a more lively or convincing colour to the Bible narrative of the sojourn in Egypt than its confident use of geographical names. To the uncritical mind a story which has a merely indefinite local background is naturally far less likely to appeal as accurate than one which names the places in which its events took place. Moreover, when, towards the close of the last century, excavators in the Eastern Delta began to announce the identification of the sites of Raamses, Pithom and Succoth, and the discovery of the exact route of the exodus, the matter seemed settled once for all, and archaeology appeared to have vindicated the geographical accuracy of the scriptural narrative.

And yet the matter is not quite so simple. It was observed that the town of Raamses, clearly named after one of the Pharaohs of that name, necessitated a Ramesside date for the exodus, a date which, although popularly accepted, clashed with the evidence of the Merenptah Victory Stela (see p. 109). It was further observed that Jacob, on his first entry into Egypt, was placed by Joseph " in the land of Rameses," a fact which would date the descent into Egypt to Ramesside times, a dating which few were prepared to accept. Moreover, quite lately it has been shown, mainly from more accurate examination of the Egyptian documents, that not all the early identifications of explorers can be accepted. It becomes therefore, necessary to examine the geography of the sojourn, and to ask firstly whether it is consistent with itself and with what we know of Egyptian geography, and secondly whether the names are contemporary with the events related and not a colouring added at a later date.

The first place-name which calls for attention is the Land of Goshen. The conception of this district existing in the mind of the compiler of the

biblical story is fortunately perfectly clear. It
is a region on the borders of Egypt, containing
good pasturage, but not occupied by the Egyptians
themselves (see especially Gen. 46.34, Ex. 8.22,
9.26). It is tempting to identify this land with
the Wadi Tumilat, the long shallow valley about
thirty miles in length, bordered by desert on
either hand and joining Egypt proper to the Suez
Canal region (Map 2). In Egyptian times, exactly
how early is uncertain, there existed in this valley
a canal which joined the Nile to the Red Sea, and
the modern railroad follows the same course.
The Septuagint translators certainly identified
this district with the land of Goshen, for the
Greek version of Gen. 46.28-29 runs : " And
he (Jacob) sent Judah before them to Joseph to
meet him at Heroonpolis," where the Hebrew
version gives the place of meeting as " the Land
of Goshen." Heroonpolis we know to have lain
in the Wadi Tumilat, and there can therefore
be no doubt as to what was in the mind of the
Greek translator. At the same time we should be
wrong in assuming that he has correctly reproduced the geographical belief of the Hebrew
compiler of the narrative. It is far from unlikely
that the Greek translator, like many of the
modern critics, has been misled by the fact that

Pithom, one of the store-cities which the Israelites built, lay in the Wadi Tumilat, into the belief that this valley was identical with Goshen. As against this there is a passage in Judith (1.7-10) in which Goshen clearly stands for the whole of the Eastern Delta, if not for the Delta in general. " And Nebuchadnezzar . . . sent unto all that dwelt in Persia, . . . and to all that were in Samaria and the cities thereof, and beyond Jordan unto Jerusalem, and Betane, and Chellus, and Kadesh, and the river of Egypt, and Tahpanes (Daphnae), and Rameses, and all the land of Goshen, until thou comest above Tanis and Memphis, and to all that dwelt in Egypt, until thou comest to the borders of Ethiopia." Here the point of view is that of one moving from Assyria through Syria down into the Eastern Delta of Egypt and on up the Nile. Clearly Egypt stands for what we now call Upper Egypt, above Memphis (near the modern Cairo), while Goshen stands for a considerable part at least of the Delta. Under these circumstances it would be well not to accept as final the view of the Septuagint, but to suppose that Goshen, though it doubtless included the Wadi Tumilat, may in the mind of the Hebrew geographer have also had a wider interpretation.

Unfortunately the whole question has been sadly obscured by an incorrect identification made many years ago by a prominent hieroglyphic scholar, Heinrich Brugsch. He originated the belief that Goshen was the same as *Gsm* (the vowels are unknown) which was supposed to be the name of a well-known ancient Egyptian town also called Pi-Sopd, the capital of the XXth nome of the Delta, which stood on the site of the modern village of Saft el-Henneh (Map 2). Despite the fact that Goshen is clearly a district and not a town, the equation seems to have been widely accepted almost without question, and it remained for Gardiner in 1918 to point out how utterly fallacious it really was. He showed that the initial consonant given by Brugsch as *G* should almost certainly be *Sh*, and clinched his argument by showing that there was very good reason why the town of Pi-Sopd, " House of the god Sopd," should also be called *Shsm*. In view of this argument and of others far too technical to be introduced here we must follow Gardiner in giving up the identification of Goshen with the town site of Saft el-Henneh, and accepting the much more natural and simple view that Goshen is a region in the Eastern Delta which includes the Wadi Tumilat, with the understanding that we have now no Egyptian authority for the name, and that it rests solely on the scriptural evidence. This conclusion appears all the more probable in view of a passage in the papyrus known as Anastasi VI, where a frontier official writes : " We have finished causing the Bedawi tribes of Edom to pass the fortress of Merenptah belonging to Theku towards the pools of Pithom (of) Merenptah belonging to Theku, in order to feed themselves and to feed their flocks." Though the event recorded here took place no earlier than the XIXth Dynasty it affords evidence that the Wadi Tumilat was a district into which foreign shepherds and their flocks were sometimes admitted.

The next geographical name to be dealt with is Raamses or Rameses. In the Hebrew version this name first occurs in Gen. 47.11, where Joseph places his father and brethren " in the land of Egypt, in the best of the land, in the land of Rameses, as Pharaoh had commanded." There is clearly a difficulty here, for a town or land called Rameses must have been named after one of the various Rameses of the XIXth and XXth Dynasties, a period far too late, on any generally accepted theory, for the entry of Jacob into Egypt. The mention of the land of Rameses is here

therefore either an error or at the best an anach-
ronism, and we may pass it over, merely remarking
that the Greek version of Gen. 46.28-29 also
mentions Rameses as the land in which Judah was
sent by Jacob to meet Joseph at the city of
Heroonpolis (see above).

In Ex. 12.11 we read " They built for Pharaoh
store cities, Pithom and Raamses," and in
Ex. 12.37, " The children of Israel journeyed from
Rameses to Succoth."   Rameses then is definitely
a town, a " store-city " as the Hebrew has it,
or a " strong city " as the more colourless Greek
translation prefers   It may be suggested that
there is no need to discuss the position of Rameses,
for Petrie has actually found it at the modern
village of Tell er-Retabeh in the Wadi Tumilat,
precisely where we should have expected it (Map
2).   Now exactly what Petrie did find at Tell
er-Retabeh is as follows : some small objects from
burials of about the IXth Egyptian Dynasty, a
temple wall bearing in relief a scene in which
Ramesses II slaughters prisoners before the god
" Tum, Lord of Theku," a stela of the same king
recording defeats inflicted on the Bedawin, a double
statue of Ramesses II and the god Tum, and some
foundation deposits of Ramesses III.   There is in
all this not a particle of evidence for identifying

this site with the biblical Raamses, and the
ancient name of the place was not recovered.[1]
Moreover, the biblical story does not make it at
all certain that Raamses lay in the Land of Goshen,
for, as several critics have pointed out, there is
a curious geographical confusion underlying the
early chapters of Exodus. At one moment the
Israelites are conceived as living aloof from the
Egyptians in the Land of Goshen, while at another
they are clearly represented as in the midst of
them. Thus the swarms of flies and the plague
of hail did not visit the Land of Goshen " where
the children of Israel were," but at the same time
Moses could " rise up in the morning and stand
before Pharaoh " ; his cradle too, deposited in the
river, was found by Pharaoh's daughter, and the
Hebrew women were instructed each woman to
" ask of her neighbour, and of her that sojourneth
in her house, jewels of silver, and jewels of gold
and raiment " ; above all, if the two races were
separated, why the need to mark the Hebrew
lintels and side-posts with blood that the Lord

---

[1] The excavator's claim that "this was a store-city of Ramessu II"
is without foundation. In an inscription found on the site is mentioned
an official among whose titles is one which the excavator mis-translates
"overseer of the granaries." In reality the title is the common "overseer
of the foreign lands." This kind of "reasoning," like that by which the
discoverer of Pithom sought to show that the place was a "store city,"
is typical of the way in which the facts of archaeology are twisted and
distorted in the service, so-called, of biblical study.

might " pass over the door." We see then that
we cannot without further enquiry assume the
town of Raamses to have been in the Wadi
Tumilat, even if this last constituted the whole of
the Land of Goshen. Nor does the occurrence of
the name in Ex. 12.11, along with that of Pithom,
which, as will be seen shortly, certainly is in the
Wadi Tumilat, lend any support to the idea, for
the passage contains not the slightest hint that the
two places were near to one another.

Now Gardiner has exhaustively examined the
Egyptian papyri and inscriptions in search of
towns in the Delta named after one or other of the
kings called Ramesses, and he finds only one with
which the Raamses-Rameses of the Bible can
conceivably be identical, and that is the town of
Pi-Ramessu, " House of Ramesses II," the Delta
capital of the XIXth Dynasty, which occupied the
site of the later Pelusium, the Avaris of the Hyksos.
In his own words " either Raamses-Rameses of
the Bible is the residence-city of the Ramessides
near Pelusium, or else it is a town unknown to
the Egyptian monuments, the existence of
which is merely postulated." If we accept his
identification the narrative becomes much more
understandable. It is clear from Ex. 12.37 and
Num. 33.3-6 that it was at Rameses that Moses

stood before Pharaoh, and from Rameses that the exodus began. It is hardly likely that Pharaoh would be in residence at some petty town in the Wadi Tumilat, which was, as we have seen, semi-foreign ground, and it is perhaps no mere coincidence that the Targum of Palestine in all the three passages where Raamses-Rameses is mentioned replaces it by Pelusin (Pelusium).

Perhaps the Psalmist was not so far from the truth when he spoke of the wonders which God performed " in the land of Egypt, in the field of Zoan," for Zoan is certainly Tanis,[1] and points to the north-east of the Delta rather than the Wadi Tumilat as the scene of Moses' activities.

Great was the satisfaction of biblical archaeologists when, in 1883, Naville, excavating at a modern village called Tell el-Maskhuteh (Map 2), discovered evidence which seemed to prove that the ancient name of that site was Pithom[2] or Pi-Tum, " House of the god Tum." From that day the

[1] The Field of Zoan was the current Egyptian name for a district somewhere in the North-east Delta.

[2] Naville's description of the ruins as those of a " store-city," enthusiastically received and repeated by many biblical archaeologists, is incorrect. The " store-chambers " which he unearthed, and which he assumed, on no evidence whatever, to extend " over the greater part of the space surrounded by the enclosure," are probably nothing more than the foundation-walls of a fortress, precisely similar to those found at Naukratis and Daphnae. These late Egyptian fortresses were built up on massive brick platforms containing hollow compartments. No one who examines Naville's plan can remain in doubt as to the real nature of what he found. Observe, too, that he discovered no evidence of the Ramesside date of this structure.

proposed identification has remained unquestioned
and once again it remained for Gardiner, in 1918,
to show that the evidence is by no means so
conclusive as had been imagined.   Let it be noted
in the first place that the Bible story gives no
more evidence for placing Pithom in the Wadi
Tumilat than it does for Raamses, though it is
clear from a rather difficult passage in the Greek
historian Herodotus that Pithom lay somewhere
on the canal which led from the Nile to the Red
Sea through the Wadi Tumilat.   It is further
clear on both traditional and linguistic grounds
that Pithom is the city known to the Greeks as
Heroonpolis, the correct original name for which
was probably Heropolis, " City of Hero," a rather
obscure god who had a temple at Magdola.
Now Naville's evidence for the identification of
Pithom-Heropolis with Tell el-Maskhuteh lies in
the fact that he found there Egyptian inscriptions
mentioning Pi-Tum, and two Latin ones mentioning Hero or Ero.   Despite this, Gardiner is
inclined to deny the identification, and to place
Pithom at Tell er-Retabeh, eight and a half miles
further west, the very site wrongly identified by
Petrie with Raamses-Rameses. He points out
that the name Pithom is found on only two
hieroglyphic inscriptions at Tell el-Maskhuteh,

while the name most frequently found there is
Theku; that Tell er-Retabeh, being a city in which
Tum was worshipped, might equally well be
regarded as Pi-Tum, " House of Tum "; that
the massive walls of Tell el-Maskhuteh suggest
very strongly the " fortress of Merenptah of
Theku " mentioned in the passage from the
papyrus Anastasi VI quoted above (p. 65), from
which it is clear that Pithom lay west of Theku;
and finally he shows that one of the two Roman
inscriptions, so far from proving that the place is
Hero or Ero rather shows that Ero lay nine
Roman miles further east. Altogether he has
made out a very strong case for the belief that
Pithom is to be looked for not at Tell el-Maskhuteh
but at Tell er-Retabeh.

The case of Succoth is fortunately much simpler.
It was Brugsch who, many years ago, first proposed
the identification with the place known from
Egyptian inscriptions as *ṯkw* (the vowels being
unknown). The identification is not perfect, for
though the *ṯ* and *k* of the Egyptian will correspond
perfectly with the Hebrew consonants which we
render *s* and *c*, the *w* of the Egyptian cannot be
rendered by *th* in Hebrew. We might, however,
suppose that, *w* being the plural ending in
Egyptian, the Hebrew authors took the word

for a plural and so rendered it by their own plural ending *oth*, thus obtaining a good Hebrew word Succoth, which means " booths," an instance of a phenomenon common in philology and known as " popular etymology." It would be foolish to pretend that this solution, though possible, is satisfactory. Had it not been for the existence in the minds of so many scholars of a preconceived notion that the Israelites left Egypt by the Wadi Tumilat it would probably never have commanded acceptance. It will shortly be seen that there is no evidence in the Bible narrative for believing that this was the route followed, and the identification of Succoth with Theku may therefore be regarded as very improbable. No other identification has up to the present been suggested.

The outcome of our enquiry into the geography of the entry into Egypt and the oppression may be briefly summed up as follows. The name Goshen is unknown from Egyptian inscriptions ; at the same time there is a district on the borders of Egypt, the Wadi Tumilat, which would answer very well to the description of the land of Goshen, and which undoubtedly formed a part if not the whole of that land. There is probably no city called after Ramesses in this district, but, as it is clear from the biblical story that the Israelites were not imagined as at all times confined to the part, we may with considerable confidence identify this town with Pi-Ramessu, the later Pelusium, the residence of the Pharaohs under the XIXth Dynasty. A town called Pithom or Pi-Tum existed in Ramesside times in the Wadi Tumilat, and is to be identified in all probability with the modern Tell er-Retabeh. Succoth is hardly likely to be identical with the Egyptian district of Theku.

The date at which the narrative was invested with this geographical colouring is manifestly not earlier than the XIXth Dynasty, from the occurrence of the town-name Rameses. This, however, need not for a moment prejudice the belief in a much earlier date for the actual sojourn. Of the geography as we have it there are two possible explanations. If tradition had preserved any geographical names from the time of the actual event the compilers would naturally replace these by their modern equivalents in cases where a change of name had taken place, as, for example, Pi-Ramessu (Rameses) for Avaris. If, on the other hand, tradition had preserved no geography of the sojourn at all, it is by no means unlikely that an editor would, in order to

increase the brightness and verisimilitude of his
narrative, introduce what appeared to him
suitable place-names from his own knowledge of
Egyptian geography, doubtless confined to a few
place-names in the Northern and Eastern Delta.
Between these two possibilities we have no means
whatsoever of deciding and we shall be wise not
to try.

The local colour of the sojourn.

Next to the use of place-names, nothing has
done more to give the narrative of the sojourn an
air of accuracy than the abundant Egyptian local
colour with which it is invested.   Again and again
this has been appealed to in proof of the historicity
of the story, and so long as our knowledge of the
history and customs of the Egyptians was in its
infancy the appeal was a strong one.   As, however,
excavation in Egypt and advancing knowledge of
the language began to enlarge our grasp of
Egyptian history, it became more and more clear
that the compiler of the narrative of the sojourn
knew less than had been imagined of the Egypt of
the period into which the sojourn, both according
to biblical chronology and external probability,

must have fallen. We have already seen that the geographical names of the sojourn, in part at least, cannot be earlier than the XIXth Dynasty, and we shall shortly find that the Egyptian names of persons mentioned in the narrative can hardly be earlier than the XXIst Dynasty.

For the moment it is necessary to deal with some of the more general aspects of the Egyptian colouring. Here it is easy to show, for example, that dreams were indeed regarded with superstitious attention in Egypt, that when Potiphar made Joseph " overseer over his house " he was entrusting to him an office which did in fact exist in the houses of the great Egyptian nobles, the office of *imi r pr ;* that the titles " chief of the butlers " and " chief of the bakers " actually occur in Egyptian inscriptions ; that Pharaoh's birthday was indeed an occasion for feasting, and possibly even for release of prisoners ; that " magicians " really existed in Egypt ; that famines did occur there ; that the signet-ring, the " vestures of fine linen " and the " gold chain about his neck " with which Pharaoh invested Joseph were fitting gifts from an Egyptian king to one whom he was in effect making his viceroy ; that the period of Joseph's life, 110 years, is the traditional length for a happy life in the Egyptian

papyri and stelae ; that the mummification of
both Jacob and Joseph was in accordance with
Egyptian custom ; that the biblical statement
" every shepherd is an abomination to the
Egyptians " is borne out, to some extent at least,
by the Egyptian evidence. It has been pointed
out, too, that the ten plagues are based on various
natural scourges known in Egypt to this day,
which perhaps occurred with particular severity
about the time of the oppression, but which
Moses ingeniously represented to Pharaoh as due
to the wrath of the god of the Hebrews, and
which later Hebrew tradition magnified until they
reached miraculous proportions. It is easy to
show all this, and more of a similar nature. And
yet the main fact which strikes the Egyptologist is
that there is nothing whatsoever in it which
suggests the Hyksos period, or indeed any particular period at all. It is all the sort of vague
general knowledge which any ancient tourist
spending a few weeks in Egypt at almost any date
after about 1600 B.C. might have acquired from
his dragoman. The references to chariots do
indeed indicate that the writer is describing a state
of things not earlier than Hyksos date, when
the horse was first introduced into Egypt. But
this is the only indication of time.

Under these circumstances, and in view of the late date of the proper names both geographical and personal, it is clear that, supposing a sojourn connected with the Hyksos movement, the local colouring must be subsequent to the events, which is merely in keeping with what we know of the composition of the Pentateuch. Instead of facing this, however, some writers have insisted on trying to show that some of this local colour is peculiarly applicable to Hyksos times or shortly later. Thus we find attempts to show that a famine did actually occur in Egypt about this period. In order to prove this, for instance, some writers quote a tomb-inscription at El Kab of one Beby, who, they state, was an official under Seqenenre III of the XVIIth Dynasty, and hence a contemporary of Joseph. This inscription contains the words " When a famine occurred for many years I gave corn to my city in each shortage." In the first place, the inscription is undated, and, though it would appear from its style to be earlier than the XVIIIth Dynasty, it cannot be fixed to any one reign or even to any one dynasty.[1] In the second place, there is no

---

[1] The dating to the reign of Seqenenre III is presumably arrived at by the totally unjustified assumption that this man Beby was the same as Baba, the father of the famous admiral Aahmes, who took part in the expulsion of the Hyksos under Aahmes I, the first king of the XVIIIth Dynasty. The admiral states that his father, Baba, served as a soldier under Seqenenre.

evidence that famines were infrequent in Egypt ;
indeed, it is on the contrary quite remarkable how
often they are mentioned on the grave stelae of
the nobles.   Thus Mentuhotp, the son of Hapi,
says : " When there came a low Nile in Year 25
I suffered not my nome to hunger.   I gave her
Upper Egyptian corn and spelt ; I allowed no
want to occur therein until high Niles came."
Similar cases could be quoted from various
periods, with such comparative frequency as to
make it manifest that any attempt to identify
some one particular famine with that mentioned
by Genesis is the merest waste of time.   All that
can be argued from the inscriptions is that
famines did occur in Egypt, a fact which we could
well have inferred from mediaeval and even
modern parallels without the need of a voice
from the dead.

Further proof of the Hyksos date of the
narrative is often said to lie in the fact that
" Joseph bought all the land of Egypt for Pharaoh :
for the Egyptians sold every man his field . . . and
the land became Pharaoh's."   Now under the
Middle Kingdom the land system of Egypt had
been a feudal one, the great nobles forming a
powerful aristocracy owning most of the land, and
threatening the power of the crown.   Under the

XVIIIth Dynasty this system has totally changed ;
these great feudal land-holders have disappeared,
and the land is vested in the king.   The explanation suggested for this change is that it was due to
Joseph's shrewd policy in buying up the land for
Pharaoh in the time of the seven years' famine.
Now quite apart from the high improbability of
this story, both as a whole and in detail, the real
explanation of the great change in the land
system which took place in Egypt between the
XIIth and XVIIIth Dynasties is perfectly well
known to us.   The invasion of the Hyksos
destroyed all rights of property in Egypt, and, as
there were no Egyptian owners, the kings who
expelled the Hyksos naturally took over the whole
of the land and disposed of it by gift or lease to
whomsoever they thought fit.   This is the true
and obvious explanation of the change which took
place in Egypt at this time.   In fact, the story of
Joseph's buying up the land is one of those stories
which tradition so frequently invents to account
for existing customs.   The custom in question is
a system of land tenure by which the Pharaoh
owned all the land except that held by the
priests, and let it out at a rental of 20 per cent. in
kind.   Unfortunately we cannot fix the date or
even the existence of such a system from our

Egyptian evidence. The Greek historians Herodotus and Diodorus Siculus speak of the land as belonging to the king, the priests and the warriors. Their evidence dates of course not earlier than the fifth century B.C., and how far back this system was in vogue it is quite impossible to say. The priests practically throughout Egyptian history held a share in the lands which were the property of the temples in which they served, and in this sense were landowners independent of the king. Gifts of lands to warriors may be traced as far back as the foundation of the XVIIIth Dynasty, though it is more probably to the assignment of lands to mercenaries in much later times that the Greek historians are referring. In short, we cannot state that the system of land tenure described in Genesis 47 is more typical of any one Egyptian period than of any other, at any rate after the Middle Kingdom (XIIth Dynasty), and we are therefore not at liberty to appeal to this system as a proof that the detail of Joseph's life is to be dated back to the Hyksos period.

There is indeed a very serious difficulty involved in any such attempt. This lies in the fact that Pharaoh marries Joseph to Asenath, daughter of Poti-pherah, priest of On. Now On is the town of Heliopolis in the Delta, and was the centre of the

Egyptian worship of Ra the Sun-god. The very
name of the priest Poti-pherah means " He whom
Ra has given." The Hyksos, who certainly
occupied the whole of the Delta and even a
considerable portion of Upper Egypt, were
worshippers of Set and, as we have seen (p. 70),
were especially hateful to the Egyptians because
" they ruled in ignorance of Ra." If we suppose
with most commentators that Joseph was a
Semite who rose to favour under a Hyksos
(Semitic) king, and that the oppression only began
after the expulsion of the Hyksos, when the
Egyptian kings of the XVIIIth Dynasty recon-
quered the Delta, we must admit that the Hyksos
king not only allowed the worship of Ra to
continue at Heliopolis, but even encouraged his
favourite Joseph to marry the daughter of Ra's
priest. All that we know of the Hyksos occupation of Egypt from the Egyptian side makes such
an admission very difficult,[1] and it is almost
beyond doubt that the story of this marriage, like
the names of the priest and his daughter, cannot
date from Hyksos times, but is a later colouring.

Before leaving this subject it is perhaps
necessary to dispel the error which is still per-

---

[1] The fact that certain Hyksos kings adopted Egyptian names compounded with Ra, does not necessarily point to a toleration of his worship.

petuated in popular books with regard to the use of straw in brick-making. It is probably based on a statement of Mr. Villiers Stuart, who visited the site of Pithom during the excavations of 1883. He says : " I carefully examined round the chamber walls, and I noticed that some of the corners of the brickwork throughout were built of bricks *without straw*. I do not remember to have met anywhere in Egypt bricks so made." The implication obviously intended is that here we have a proof of the accuracy of the Bible narrative, for here in the walls of Pithom, a store-city built by the Hebrew bondmen, are the very bricks which they were forced to make without straw. It is almost inconceivable that any traveller in Egypt should make this statement with regard to the use of straw in bricks, for though straw has been used both in ancient and modern times, its use is somewhat rare, more particularly in ancient times. What is more, the writer of this passage in the narrative is certainly under some strange delusion as to the function of the straw when used. Its purpose is to bind the mud more tightly together, though as a matter of fact the Nile mud coheres so well of itself that no binding material is really necessary. Consequently the refusal of the task-masters to provide the Israelites with straw would not in the slightest degree increase the difficulty of their labours. As a piece of local colour the whole incident is unsatisfactory, and goes to prove the writer's ignorance of Egyptian customs rather than his close acquaintance with them, as is so often averred.[1]

The personal names of the sojourn.

For many years biblical students insisted on believing that the names Potiphar, Poti-pherah, Asenath and Zaphenathpaneah were good Egyptian names of the Hyksos period or there-abouts, and it is only quite lately that the efforts of Egyptian philologists have really succeeded in dispelling this illusion, which, indeed, still lingers on in the minds of the uncritical. Potiphar and Potipherah are two spellings of a common Egyptian name which means " He whom Ra has given." Names of the type " He whom such and such a god has given " are unknown in Egypt before the XXIst Dynasty, and do not become at

---

[1] The ingenious suggestion of one writer that the chopped straw was used to spread on the hands and floor and moulds, in order to prevent the wet bricks from sticking and thus delaying the worker, is not supported by modern or, as far as we know, by ancient usage in Egypt. Chopped straw is, however, used for a similar purpose by the modern potters.

all frequent before the XXIInd, roughly the ninth
and eighth centuries B.C. Naville, anxious to
escape the consequences involved by the late date
of such names in Egypt, interprets Potiphar and
Potipherah as being separate names derived from
the Egyptian *p-ḥotep-ḥar* " the gift or offering
of Horus," and *p-ḥotep-reʿ* "the gift or offering
of Ra" respectively. Quite apart from various
grammatical difficulties involved this explanation
is ruled out by the absence of the *ḥ* of *ḥotep* in
the Hebrew equivalents, and by the fact that
names of this type are totally unknown in Egypt,
the word *ḥotep* never bearing the meaning of
" gift " in the sense in which a child could be
said to be (and therefore named) " The gift of Ra."
Asenath is an Egyptian name meaning " Belonging
to the goddess Neit." Names of this type are
not absolutely wanting in the earlier periods,
but they are extremely rare, and it is only in the
XXIst Dynasty that they begin to be common.
Zaphenathpaneah has been explained with a
very high degree of probability as an attempt
to render in Hebrew an Egyptian name meaning
" The god spoke and he (the child) lived."
This is the only interpretation of the name
which is free from objections, either phonetic or
grammatical, and the correspondence between

Egyptian and Hebrew is so striking that there is hardly room for doubt. Names of this type are absent in Egypt until the end of the XXth Dynasty and do not become usual until the XXIInd. Some object to this explanation on the ground that what the sense here requires is not an ordinary proper name, but some specially honorific title conferred on Joseph for his services. To these it may be replied that this inconsistency, instead of being used to discredit the explanation of the name here offered, can just as well be used as evidence for the inaccurate nature of the Egyptian colouring supplied to the narrative by the compilers of the ninth and eighth centuries B.C.[1]

Thus the three Egyptian proper names of persons in the Joseph narrative are all seen to be of types frequent in the XXIInd Dynasty, but very rare or even wanting in earlier periods. The conclusion cannot be avoided that the colouring which gave these names to the narrative

[1] Naville's very attractive suggestion that the word means "Head of the *per ankh*" or "College of Learning" is ruled out by the fact that, on his hypothesis, the *th* in the Hebrew rendering would require the first word to be feminine. This word, therefore, cannot be the masculine *ṭsw* "a commander" or "leader" but only *ṭst* "a body of men" (especially soldiers). In the example which he quotes from Bubastis to prove that the feminine *ṭst* can be used for the masculine *ṭsw* in the sense of "head" or "leader" Naville has failed to observe that the phrase *ṭst nt pr ʿnḫ* refers not to one person but to a group of persons, so that *ṭst* here means not the "head" but the "staff" or "personnel."

is not earlier than the ninth century B.C., that
is to say about the time of the writing of documents J and E.   It would be difficult to say
whether the whole of the local colour is to be
attributed to one period.   The general atmos-
phere we have already seen to be so vague that
we cannot refer it to its place in Egyptian history,
while the geographical detail is clearly not earlier
than Ramesside times (XIXth to XXth Dynasty).

The Egyptian words actually used in the
Hebrew of the Joseph story give us no help whatever.   In the first place they are all words which
were commonly used in Hebrew, and which
occur in other passages of the Old Testament ;
and in the second place they are all words which
had a very long life in Egyptian and can be taken
to point to no one period more than any other.
They are four in number ; *Pharaoh*, literally
" The Great House," commonly used as an
official designation of the King from the XVIIIth
Dynasty onward ; *ye'ōr*, the usual Hebrew name
for the Nile, meaning in Egyptian " a stream " ;
āḥū, meaning " reed-grass," and *shesh*, meaning
" fine linen."

To these is possibly to be added the *abrech* of
Genesis 41.43 (A.V. marginal rendering).   Of the

various theories advanced as to the origin of this word the most attractive is that which sees in it the Semitic word to " bow the knee." On the other hand, Spiegelberg's suggestion that it is the Egyptian expression *ib rk* used in the sense of " Look out " merits serious consideration, though the examples he quotes cannot quite be said to establish the use of the phrase in precisely the sense here needed.

CHAPTER V

Date of the exodus

A HISTORIAN who proposed to discuss the date
and geography of the siege of Troy would begin
by satisfying himself that such an event actually
occurred, and by striving to ascertain its true
nature.   In the same way, it is useless to try to fix
the date and the route of the exodus unless we have
first satisfied ourselves that it really happened, and
then made every effort to discover its nature and
the scale on which it occurred.   Thus, for instance,
if the exodus consisted or appeared to consist of
the departure from Egypt of some 70 souls, the
same number as those who originally entered
Egypt, living apart in a remote corner of the
Eastern Delta, it would be almost useless to look
for any record of such a pigmy movement in the
Egyptian sources ; whereas, if the numbers of the
emigrants were nearly 2,000,000, which is a
legitimate deduction from Exodus 12.37, the
movement was one which would have shaken

Egypt to its very foundation, and which, even if it had failed to be recorded in one of the numerous monuments which have survived in Egypt, would at any rate have left some unmistakable impression on Egyptian history.

That an exodus occurred need not for a moment be doubted. It has already been pointed out that the whole incident of the sojourn in Egypt is bound up so closely with the revelation of Jehovah that it is hardly likely to be a pure invention. If, then, some of the ancestors of the later Israelites were once in Egypt they must at some moment have come out of it, and therefore there must have been an exodus.

But when we come to the nature and scale of the movement, difficulties beset us on every side. The biblical account as we have it dates from long after the event, and is clearly heavily biassed on the Hebrew side. The point of view of the later Israelites was that Yahweh had brought them out of Egypt " with an high hand," and the account was written with the express object of illustrating this. We must therefore be prepared to reject as later embellishment much of the story as it appears in the Book of the Exodus, and to imagine the actual event as of a much more humble nature. As for the numbers of the Israelites we cannot for

a moment entertain a belief in the two millions[1]
suggested by Ex. 12.37. It is incredible that
this vast people could have maintained themselves
in the desert between Egypt and Canaan for the
forty years demanded by tradition, and extremely
doubtful, in the light of modern experience,
whether they could even have made the direct
march from Egypt to Kadesh.

The exodus when reduced to its proper proportions becomes an event which may well have
left no trace in Egyptian history, and any attempts
to fix its date and its route must unfortunately be
based mainly on *a priori* evidence.

If there is one firmly rooted idea in the popular
mind with regard to the exodus it is that the
Pharaoh under whom it took place was King
Merenptah of the XIXth Dynasty, who ruled
from about 1225 to 1215 B.C. Even the discovery
of the king's mummy safely reposing in a tomb at
Thebes failed to shake the belief, for it was pointed
out that, though the biblical narrative states that
the Pharaoh and all his chariots were overwhelmed
in the Red Sea, there is no reason why his body

---

[1] It has been suggested that these high numbers might be greatly
reduced by translating the word *alaf*, generally rendered " thousands," by
" families." Thus, in place of the 46,500 of the tribe of Reuben we should
get " the 46 families of the tribe of Reuben, numbering in all 500 " and
so on, giving a total of 5550. Hebrew scholars, however, are not prepared
to admit that the word *alaf* could in a passage of this nature bear the meaning
of " families " here attributed to it.

should not have been recovered and brought back to Thebes for burial. Enthusiasts have even gone so far as to attempt to show from the condition of the mummy that the king died from drowning.

The evidence for the belief that Merenptah was the Pharaoh of the exodus, nevertheless, can only be described as so flimsy that it is difficult to see how the belief can ever have arisen. If analysed impartially it amounts to nothing more than the facts that the Pharaoh of the oppression has generally been assumed to be Ramesses II, and that Merenptah succeeded him. The identification of Ramesses II with the oppressor is based merely on the statement that under the oppression the Israelites " built for Pharaoh store cities, Pithom and Raamses." It was assumed, quite rightly, that Raamses must have been named after a king, and that, as Ramesses I was an ephemeral king who did very little building, the probable founder of the city was Ramesses II. Now we have already seen (pp. 82 ff.) that this evidence proves nothing, since the geographical names of the sojourn are much later than the period at which the events took place; because the town which the Israelites built was called Raamses in, say, 900 B.C. it does not for a moment follow that it was so called when the Israelites

built it, and therefore we may not argue that this
building, which incidentally need not mean the
original foundation, took place as late as the reign
of Ramesses II, or for the matter of that
Ramesses I.

This popular hypothesis of an exodus under
Merenptah was, curious to relate, regarded by
many as established fact when the great
Merenptah Victory Stela was discovered at Thebes
by Petrie in 1896.   Not later than the fifth year
of his reign Merenptah conducted, or at least
organized, a campaign against Palestine, to the
successful results of which he refers in an inscription recording his Libyan war, on the back of
a large black granite stela set up by an earlier
conqueror, Amenhotp III of the XVIIIth
Dynasty.   At the end of the lengthy song of
triumph occur the sentences " Canaan is captured
with every evil circumstance (?).   Askalon is
carried captive.   Gezer is taken.   Yenoam is
brought to nought.   Israel is destroyed, its seed
is not.   Syria has become as the widows of Egypt.
All the lands together are at peace."   It is almost
incredible that in some minds the discovery of this
new document merely served to clinch the belief
in the dating of the exodus to the reign of
Merenptah.   Cooler heads, however, were much

more concerned to note that, so far from con-
firming the Merenptah date it made it practically
impossible, for obviously, if the Israelites left
Egypt in Merenptah's own reign and wandered
forty years before reaching Canaan, he could
hardly have found them settled there as early as
his fifth year. Some would avoid the difficulty
by supposing that the Israel tribe whom
Merenptah attacked in Canaan were either
Israelites who had never descended into Egypt[1]
with Jacob, or a portion who had left Egypt before
the biblical exodus, and find confirmation of this
in the fact that in certain lists of Syrian places
dating from the reigns of Seti I and Ramesses II,
the predecessors of Merenptah, we find a district
mentioned whose consonants are identical with
those of the Hebrew tribe Asher. Some have
gone so far as to attempt to show that this
district, judging by its position among the names
in the lists, lay precisely in the position known to
have been occupied by the tribe Asher in the time
of the judges. Their arguments, however, are
far from convincing, and the identity of the place

---

[1] That there were such they would argue from the occurrence in a list
of southern Syrian towns dating from the reign of Thothmes III, about
1480 B.C., of two town-names which appear to read Jacob-el and Joseph-el
respectively, though with regard to the reading of the second there is great
uncertainty. The existence of towns in Syria with these names, if the readings
be correct, is certainly a warning against the assumption that *the whole* of
the people later known as the Israelites necessarily descended into Egypt.

mentioned by Seti and Ramesses with the Asher of the biblical story must be regarded as most doubtful.

In any case, it is hardly worth while going to all this trouble to defend the theory of an exodus under Merenptah, for which there is so little to be said on other grounds.[1] Is there no earlier date at which, in view of Egyptian and Syrian history, an exodus might reasonably have fallen ? Let us take the Hebrews' own chronology, and, without assuming its accuracy, see whether it will furnish us with a useful and reasonable indication.

We are told in I Kings 6.1 that the building of the temple in Solomon's fourth year took place 480 years after the exodus. Now we can date Solomon's reign very accurately, for the battle of Qarqar, at which Ahab was present in alliance with Hadad-idri of Damascus, the Benhadad II of I Kings 20.33, as related by the Assyrian account of it, can be fixed astronomically to 854 B.C. This alliance seems to have been made in Ahab's twenty-first year, and, by reckoning backward over a period the documentary sources for which are in part at least contemporary and should

---

[1] Eerdmans' startling suggestion that the descent into Egypt did not take place until after the reign of Merenptah is worthy of mention in passing, though from the biblical point of view the chronological difficulties involved are quite insuperable.

therefore be worthy of considerable credit, we get 970 B.C. for Solomon's accession,[1] and 966 for the building of the temple. Adding 480 to this we obtain 1446 B.C. for the traditional date of the exodus. Now we must not assign to this 480 years, which, like Assyrian numbers of precisely the same type, is nothing more than a round figure, more importance than it can bear ; at the same time it is worthy of note that if the exodus took place under Merenptah, who came to the throne in 1225 B.C., then Hebrew tradition has made an error of about 230 years, or nearly half the whole figure, an error which, though not inconceivable in dealing with very remote events, is a little unlikely in dealing with comparatively recent times.

Let us then take this date 1446 B.C., and ask whether it is for any reason a probable date for an exodus. The reigning king in Egypt at this date was Amenhotp II, who succeeded Thothmes III, the great conqueror who had carried the Egyptian arms through Palestine and Syria up into the Lebanon, and even on to the upper reaches of the Euphrates. The vast Asiatic Empire thus founded had been maintained

---

[1] We have of course to assume the rather suspicious 40 years given as the length of Solomon's reign.

more or less intact through the reigns of
Amenhotp II, Thothmes IV and Amenhotp III.
To the last of this great line of kings succeeded,
however, the strange individual known as
Akhenaton. He was the son of his predecessor on
the throne and of his queen Ty, who, though she
may have inherited some slight strain of Asiatic
blood on the mother's side, cannot rightly be
described, as she sometimes has been, as a
" foreigner." Not later than the sixth year of
his reign the young king, then apparently still in
his teens, had effected a religious revolution in the
state. He had moved his capital from Thebes,
where it had stood for centuries, down the Nile
to a desolate spot near the modern village of
et-Til, a spot to which Europeans have given the
misnomer of Tell el-Amarna. Here he set to
work to erect on virgin ground a new city called
Akhetaton, the Horizon of the Disk, in which he
might devote himself to the worship of the Sun's
Disk or Aton, a deity already existent but
insignificant, whose worship he had established as
the state religion in Egypt. From Amenhotp,
" Amon is satisfied," he changed his own name to
Akhenaton, " The Disk is pleased," and he
completely suppressed the numerous gods whom
his fathers had been wont to serve.

H

With the causes of this revolution we have here no concern ; our business is rather with its results. Occupied in beautifying Akhetaton and in inditing hymns to the Disk, the young king appears to have completely neglected politics both internal and external. A happy chance has preserved to us the archives of the Foreign Office at Akhetaton, for in 1887 a peasant-woman, searching among the ruins, unearthed a large number of clay tablets inscribed almost without exception in Babylonian cuneiform. These tablets proved on examination to form the diplomatic correspondence which passed between the kings of Egypt, Akhenaton and his father, and the various rulers and dynasts of Syria and other parts of Nearer Asia with regard to political events of the utmost importance to Egypt which were then happening in Syria and Palestine. From these letters we can see that while Akhenaton played and sang the Egyptian Empire in Asia was tottering to its downfall. In the north, in Syria proper, the subject rulers of various city states were in open revolt against Egypt, with the connivance and encouragement of the Hittites, a people who had already established a great kingdom in Asia Minor and were anxious to overrun Syria (Map 1). In Palestine an equally serious state of things existed, and, while some of

the rulers were already in revolt, others, along with
the governors left in some cases by the Egyptians
themselves, were appealing desperately for help
against the inroads of a people called the Khabiru.
Abdakhiba, the governor left by the Egyptians in
Jerusalem writes (Letter 181) " The whole of the
king's land, which has begun hostilities against me,
will be lost. Behold the land of Seir as far as
Carmel, its princes are wholly lost, and hostility
prevails against me. There remains not one
prince to my lord the king, every one is ruined.
Let the king take care of his land and send troops,
for if no troops come this year the whole territory
of my lord the king will perish."

Are these Khabiru the Hebrews, and are we to
see in the state of things revealed in Palestine the
Syrian version of the entry of the tribes under
Joshua ? These questions, for they are two and
not one and the same, have formed the centre of
one of the most vehement discussions in biblical
archaeology, and the best scholars are completely
divided in opinion on the matter.

Firstly, then, are the Khabiru the Hebrews ?
The spelling of Khabiru which we find in the
cuneiform letters is a perfectly sound phonetic
equivalent for Hebrews. The initial letter of the
word Hebrew which we write as an H is in reality

not an H, but the Semitic guttural *'ain*, which European languages do not possess. Babylonian, too, was wanting in this sound, and in writing foreign proper names it substituted for it a *kh*. Philologically, then, the identification of the Khabiru with the Hebrews is unexceptionable. This proves nothing in itself, for it is always possible, though not very probable, that two totally different peoples should have existed whose names were so closely alike as to contain precisely the same consonants written in precisely the same order. Thus, though we cannot prove it, we are left with the feeling that the identification of the Khabiru with the Hebrews of Bible history is far from unlikely.

If this identification is right, and the Khabiru are the Hebrews, are these Hebrews either wholly or partially identical with the tribes who came out of Egypt ? This problem can obviously only be attacked by examining the Tell el-Amarna letters with a view to discovering the nature and magnitude of the Khabiru-movement, and then asking whether this movement can be equated with the entry into Canaan of the people of the exodus. In order to do this it is first necessary to clear up the identity of a people spoken of in the letters as Sagaz. They occur both in the letters referring

to the northern part of Syria and in those referring
to Palestine proper, always as a force hostile to
the present occupants of the cities. One of the
tablets contains what is known as a syllabary, that
is to say, a dictionary of difficult words or signs,
in which the ideogram which we render Sagaz is
explained as equivalent to *khab-b(atum)*, which
means robber, and in another tablet a marginal
note or gloss explains it as *khab-ba-a-te*. Moreover, the Babylonian verb *shagashu* means to slay
or destroy. From this Burney concludes that
the ideogram Sagaz was read and understood
as *khabbatum*, "the robber people." Now
Abdakhiba, governor of Jerusalem, speaks in his
letters to Egypt of the invading Khabiru, while
other princes in Palestine never mention Khabiru
but only Sagaz. It is hard to escape the conclusion that Khabiru and Sagaz are two names for
one and the same people, and this is supported in
remarkable fashion by an inscription found at
Boghaz Keui, the Hittite capital in Asia Minor,
in which the phrase " Khabiru-gods " is used as
an equivalent for " Sagaz-gods."

Now if this identification of Sagaz with
Khabiru be accepted it carries in its train an
important corollary. The Khabiru-Sagaz attacks
were not limited to Palestine, but also affected

Syria further to the north; it would therefore
seem difficult to identify this movement *as a whole*
with the entry of the tribes under Joshua into
Canaan, which, as is abundantly clear from the
Bible narrative, affected only a limited area within
Palestine. Burney accepts the logical consequences
involved and definitely dissociates the Khabiru
from that group of the Hebrews who entered
Canaan under Joshua. He would connect the
Khabiru movement with the third of those vast
migrations of Semitic peoples from their original
home, possibly in Arabia, to which reference was
made in Chapter I, that of the Aramaeans.
He points out that in the marriage of Isaac with
Rebekah we have a traditional connection between
the Hebrews and the Aramaeans, Rebekah's
brother being an inhabitant of Padan-aram.
He therefore regards the Khabiru who invaded
Canaan in Akhenaton's time as descendants of the
original Hebrews who had settled in Canaan in
Abram's days, been afterwards crowded out over
the Jordan, and were now again entering borne on
the stream of the immigration of the Aramaeans,
to whom they were closely akin.

This is not the place to discuss in full such a
theory, and in any case our almost complete
ignorance of the early history and movements of

the Aramaeans would render discussion almost futile. Nevertheless, Burney's view should warn us not to accept too lightly the proposed identification of Khabiru with the tribes under Joshua. Excavation in Palestine is still in its infancy, and we are certainly not yet in a position to deny the possibility of some such explanation as Burney has given.

At the same time it is possible that the correct view lies in a compromise. If the Khabiru-Sagaz are not *as a whole* identical with the Hebrews from Egypt they may be so in part. Is it perhaps significant that we never hear of Khabiru in the northern part of Syria, but that they are mentioned only in the letters of Abdikhiba of Jerusalem ? In other words, is it not possible that the Hebrews under Joshua, after reaching the east of Jordan, combined with other elements of allied race in a united attack on the whole of Syria-Palestine, the Joshua-group forming the southern wing of this huge immigration ? Here again is a question which we cannot answer, but which it is not improbable that archaeology will be in a position to answer after another decade or two of systematic excavation in Syria.

The results of this investigation are disappointingly negative. At every point we are baulked by lack of sufficient information. Egyptian sources never mention the Israelites; the Tell el-Amarna letters do mention a people who may be Hebrews, but who, even in this case, need not be those Hebrews who came out of Egypt. The biblical sources do not give us the means of settling the point raised by the letters, for we never discern there what is the relation of the tribes of the exodus to the twelve tribes after-wards known as Israel. Only one thing is clear, namely, that the exodus from Egypt did not include the whole of these latter.

In the absence of sound evidence scholars have allowed themselves to be swayed by slight indications. The two main schools of thought are those which identify the Khabiru, or a part of them, with the Hebrews of the exodus, thus obtaining a date of about 1400 B.C., for this event, and those who believe that the building by the Israelites of the " store city " of Rameses dates the oppression to Ramesses II and the exodus to his successor Merenptah, about 1220 B.C. Neither school has the evidence to prove its case, and both may well be wrong. If the Khabiru-school argue " Our hypothesis fits in admirably with the biblical chronology, while yours would reduce the 480 years of I Kings 6.1 to half, and condense the

period of the Judges into 250 years," the
Merenptah-school reply " We may do violence to
biblical chronology, which is a thing of very
uncertain value. You, however, do worse. You
ask us to believe that the period of the Judges
covers the years between 1400 and 1000 B.C., and
that although Israel was in Canaan all this time
yet her records have not preserved a single hint
of those numerous campaigns which the great
Egyptian conquerors Seti I, Ramesses II,
Merenptah and Ramesses III carried out in
Palestine and Syria during those four centuries."

Surely it is not pusillanimous to refuse to
identify oneself with either of these two schools so
long as neither can produce evidence which would
be seriously listened to in a court of law, and so
long as a dozen other solutions are equally possible
a priori. Still, where reason fails feeling always
comes in, and the writer is bound to confess to
a feeling of greater antipathy to the Merenptah
date than to the earlier. The argument that had
the Israelites been in Canaan during the period of
the great Egyptian expeditions of the XIXth and
XXth Dynasties, urged with such plausibility by
Burney, loses its force when we read the same
scholar's own account of the extremely artificial
composition of the Book of Judges, which consists

mainly in a collection of incidents arranged by an editor in such a fashion as to show that defection from the worship of Yahweh invariably led to deliverance into the hand of foreign enemies, and that the ensuing repentance was followed by the raising up of a deliverer. The illustrations of this principle " are, at any rate in most cases, merely *local*, some particular tribe or group of tribes falling temporarily under the dominion of a foreign oppressor, but Israel as a whole being unaffected." Surely in such a narrative as this, compiled long after the events, we can argue nothing from the absence of any reference to Egyptian invasions. These invasions, rapid and far-reaching, probably in many cases had but little effect on any part of Israel, and the fact that they have left no record in an account which by admission makes no claim to completeness hardly amounts to evidence. That the Khabiru school can cite in their favour the agreement of their chronology with that of I Kings 6.1 is probably a matter of very little importance, and those who resent " criticism " may well be allowed a malicious smile when they find a German adherent of the Khabiru theory defending the 300 years of Judges 11.26 as older than the framework in which it is set and therefore of value, while a great

British biblical scholar, an ardent follower of the
Merenptah theory, condemns it as a late and
worthless interpolation.

It is impossible to leave this part of the subject
without a reference to the famous Aperu or Aperiu
of the Egyptian monuments, whom some authorities have tried to identify with the oppressed
Hebrews.   The word is written in Egyptian with
the consonants *prw* or *pryw*, the *w* being merely
the plural ending, the ‘ representing the Semitic
guttural *ain*, and the vowels of course being
unwritten and therefore unknown.   The word
occurs five times, four times determined by the
signs determining a foreign people, once by those
used to indicate a foreign land.   In the passage
from the Papyrus Harris 500, written during the
XXth Dynasty and containing a folk-story about
the siege of Joppa under Thothmes III, it is
difficult to determine from the damaged context
whether the Aperiu belong to the Egyptian army
or to the inhabitants of Joppa, the former being
the more probable.   The passage throws no light
on their functions.   In two papyri in the Museum
of Leyden, of the time of Ramesses II, these people
are represented as engaged in dragging up stone
for temples built by Ramesses.   In the great

Harris Papyrus (Ramesses III) certain Aperu are mentioned as belonging to a temple endowment together with " sons of foreign chiefs " and " Maryn " (Syrian warriors of some kind). Finally in the time of Ramesses IV we find on a rock stela in the quarries of the Hammamat valley that " 800 Aperu of the Anu-troops "[1] took part in an expedition thither.

Are these people the Hebrews ?   Their position as forced labourers in the Leyden Papyri passages make this theory extremely attractive.   On the other hand, there is a slight philological difficulty, for the Semitic word for a Hebrew ought to be rendered in Egyptian not by *'pr* but by *'br*. It is true that rare examples exist where Hebrew *b* is represented by Egyptian *p*, but it is a large assumption to suppose that this is one of such cases. Chronologically the difficulty is practically insuperable.   With the exception of Eerdmans no scholar postulates a later date than the reign of Merenptah for the exodus, and yet there are still Aperu in Egypt in the reigns of Ramesses III and IV, which bring us down to 1160 B.C.   If the Aperu are the Hebrews we must either adopt Eerdmans' theory that the Israelites only entered

---

[1] The text is damaged here and the translation is therefore not quite certain.

Egypt after the fifth year of Merentpah, or we must suppose that some of the Hebrews remained in Egypt after the exodus of the main body, a supposition which, though the biblical narrative lends no colour to it, some scholars, notably Driver, are prepared to accept. If the philological equivalence of Hebrew and Aper were perfect there would be much to be said for this conclusion, but, as it is not, it would seem safer to refuse to accept on present evidence the identity of the two peoples.

Route of the exodus

The question of the route of the exodus has proved a happy playing-field for the amateur. The reason is, as always in such cases, that it is a field where it is extremely difficult either to prove or to disprove anything at all, so that the sage and the fool may work in it almost on level terms. Even in the more scholarly discussions of the subject one point of vital importance is almost always overlooked. The whole geography of the sojourn in Egypt is, as has been demonstrated in the last chapter, anachronistic, having been imposed on the original tradition long after the events themselves. Thus we are not in a position to discover what route the Israelites really followed, except in so far as we may conjecture it by the application of common sense to the problem. All we can hope to recover is the route which the compilers of the ninth century B.C. and onward thought that they followed, which is a very different thing. Having premised so much we can now proceed to our problem.

For practical purposes it will be convenient to reverse the natural order of events, by asking first what was the general direction of the exodus as imagined by the compilers of the narrative, and only afterwards returning to the more detailed question of the precise route by which the emigrants left Egypt, the answer to which depends to a great extent on our answer to the former.

In the first place, we may clear the ground by noticing that the peninsula now known as Sinai only acquired that name in comparatively modern times. Modern research has shown that the attaching of this name to the peninsula, and more particularly the identification of the biblical Mt. Sinai with a certain mountain in the south of it can only be traced back to about the third century A.D., when certain colonies of Christians who lived there, anxious to increase the importance of their home, made it the scene of the wanderings of the Israelites. It follows from this that whatever view we take of the geographical names of the biblical story of the exodus we are not justified in placing any of them in the peninsula merely because it now goes by the name of Sinai. The Christians of Sinai might, of course, have been right in their identification, but on the other hand they might equally well have been wrong, and in the sequel it will appear that they probably were.

The narrative of the exodus contains a very large number of geographical names, hardly one of which can, with complete certainty, be identified with any known locality, and leaves us in total darkness as to the scene of the wanderings from the moment of leaving Egypt to the moment of arriving at the Jordan. Wildernesses and deserts are multiplied ; we have the wilderness of Shur, the wilderness of Sin, the wilderness of Sinai, the wilderness of Zin and the wilderness of Paran, and at first sight it would seem impossible to make anything of the confusion. If, however, the reader will take a marked Bible and read only those passages in the story of the exodus which are derived from the oldest document, J, he will find that the narrative, far from being confused, is remarkably straightforward. The Israelites leave Egypt and march direct across to Kadesh. This place is almost certainly to be identified with the oasis of 'Ain Gadis on the southern borders of Palestine, a place distinguished in modern times as having been for some time the railhead of the Turkish army in its attack on Egypt during the war. If we suppose that the Israelites left Egypt with any definite idea of their destination it would seem extremely probable that J has given a correct if summary account of their movements.

From Kadesh[1] the Israelites make a pilgrimage to Mount Sinai, where the commandments are given to them. This must be a primitive sanctuary of Yahweh. But where does it lie? Much depends on the meaning of Deut. 33.2, " The Lord came from Sinai, and rose from Seir unto them : he shined forth from mount Paran, and came from Meribath-Kadesh." Unfortunately it is uncertain whether the original read " from " or " to " Meribath-Kadesh, and thus the conclusions to be drawn from the passage are uncertain. In Judges 5.4 Yahweh is represented as coming to the assistance of his people from

---

[1] Some critics think that J combines two versions, in the earlier of which the law is given by Yahweh *at Kadesh itself*. The question is immaterial for our investigation.

Seir and Edom : " in thy progress from Seir, in
thy march from the field of Edom." In the
passage from Deut. 33.2 Seir and Mount Paran
would appear to be in Yahweh's course. The
prayer of Habakkuk tells us that " God came from
Teman, and the holy one from Mount Paran."
Here Teman, literally the right hand side or south
country, refers, as is clear from Ezekiel 25.13 and
Obadiah 9, to a part of Edom. Now Seir is the
mountain range which runs southward from the
Dead Sea towards the Gulf of Akaba, and Edom
is the country round about that range. These
indications would place Sinai somewhere in or
near Edom and not very far from Kadesh, with
which it is moreover closely connected in the
narratives. Such a position seems quite consistent with all that we learn of Sinai in the Old
Testament. Any attempt to reach greater
precision meets with difficulties. Some, for
instance, would place the mountain actually
east of the Gulf of Akaba. They believe, and
there is much to be said for it, that the close
connection between Moses and Yahweh is due
to his relations with Jethro the Midianite priest.
The Greek geographer, Ptolemy, and the Arabic
writers mention a place called Modiana or
Madyan in Arabia, east of the Gulf of Akaba,

I

and this place may mark the original site of the Midianite country, and therefore of Sinai the sacred mountain of Yahweh. Others would place Mount Sinai much nearer to Kadesh, on the western border of Edom. To this it may be objected, that in Deuteronomy 1.2, Horeb is said to be no less than 11 days' journey from Kadesh. Now Horeb, in Document E, appears to answer in every respect to Sinai in J, and is generally assumed to be another name for the sacred mountain, and if this is right then Sinai-Horeb is 11 days' journey from Kadesh and can hardly be as near it as the west border of Edom. But the criticism is not very cogent, for the fact that E calls the sacred mountain Horeb while J calls it Sinai may mean that the two sources preserved traditions differing not only in the name given to the mountain but in the geographical position assigned to it.

It is hardly necessary to go more deeply into a question which is doubtless beyond solution, indeed our intention in going so far has been merely to insist on the total absence of any serious evidence for the placing of Mount Sinai in the Sinai Peninsula, and for its having been identified by the compilers of the Bible narrative with any particular

mountain there, such as Gebel Musa or Gebel
Serbal.

So much for the simple narrative of Document
J. If the passages due to E are now examined
it will be seen that a new episode is introduced
into the story after the passage of the Sea of
Reeds, namely the visit to Marah and Elim[1]
(Ex. 15.22-27). Is this compatible with the
narrative of J, or does it represent a separate
tradition ? Those who accept as the original
and correct version the simple story of J have
no difficulty in placing Marah and Elim between
Egypt and Kadesh, actually identifying Elim
with the Eloth of I Kings 9.26, the modern
Akaba at the head of the gulf (Map 1). Others,
however, have placed Marah and Elim near the
west coast of the peninsula of Sinai, and an
enormous amount of ingenuity has been expended
on trying to find sites which will answer to the
conditions required. This anxiety to place these
two sites on the west of Sinai is due partly to
the inability of scholars to cut their minds loose
from the Christian tradition of the fourth
century A.D., which fixed the peninsula as the
scene of the wanderings and actually marked out

1. Some critics assign this episode to J. If this is correct the question
discussed here does not arise.

a route for the edification of pilgrims, partly to a curious indication in the itinerary as given by the latest document, P, to which we must now turn. In Numbers 33 P follows the route of the combined JE from Rameses through Succoth, Etham, Pi-hahiroth and Migdol to Marah and Elim. Then follows a return to the Sea of Reeds, after which is a long list of place names not one of which can be identified until we reach Ezion-geber and Kadesh. For those who suppose an exodus *via* the Wadi Tumilat, with a crossing of some ancient extension of the Red Sea, now dried up, this return to the Sea of Reeds (which, with the Septuagint, they persist in identifying with the Red Sea) can hardly mean anything other than that the people had now reached some spot near the west coast of the Sinai Peninsula, from whence they turned down to the Red Sea, *i.e.* east side of the Gulf of Suez. This once fixed there was no difficulty in finding suitable spots for Marah and Elim. A century ago Burckhardt had identified Marah with the well of Hawwarah, 47 miles S.E. of 'Ain Musa and 7 miles from the coast, on the modern path from Egypt to Gebel Musa, a well so brackish as to be almost unfit to drink. 'Ain Naba, 10 miles south-east of Suez, has also been suggested.

Similarly Elim was identified by Burckhardt with
a spot in the Wady Gharandel, while others find it
in 'Ain Musa, 6 miles south-west of 'Ain Naba.
The Middle Ages were not without their identifications, for early travellers were shown at
Klysma the spot where the Red Sea was crossed,
at 'Ain Musa the site of the bitter spring of
Marah, and in the oasis of the Wady Gharandel
the springs and the palm trees of Elim. Further
towards the south the town of Faran was shown
to them as the site of Rephidim, and so the
journey continued until it reached its climax
at the foot of the " sacred mountain."

Such is the process by which the simple
account of J, involving nothing more than a
direct journey from Egypt to Kadesh, has been
enlarged and mishandled by critics both ancient
and modern until it has developed into a round-
about wandering through the mountainous
regions of the peninsula of Sinai. For those who
have time it may be a pleasing occupation to
identify the various sites in the route of the
exodus with places in this district, but those
who do it should do it with their eyes open to
the fact that not a single place name in J, E or
P can with certainty, or even with probability,
be placed there, and that in none of these narra-

tives is there, for an unprejudiced mind, the
slightest indication that the scene of the exodus
lay so far to the south.

The route of the earlier part of the exodus,
namely the journey from Rameses into the
wilderness, though not simple, is far less complicated than that of the wanderings. Document
P alone gives geographical names and details.
The writer, though he lives 800 or 1000 years
after the events, whatever they were, which gave
rise to the story of an exodus, has at any rate
some kind of geographical scheme in his mind.
This scheme has been completely obscured by
the obstinacy of critics in insisting on an exodus
by way of the Wadi Tumilat, for which there is
not a particle of evidence. The mistake, however, was not unnatural, and had its rise in the
fixing of the site of Pithom in that region. It
was next assumed that Rameses-Raamses must
be near Pithom, and that the two must be in
Goshen, which must therefore be the Wadi
Tumilat. This assumption once made, it was
natural to suppose that the Hebrews left Egypt
via this valley, and the matter seemed beyond
doubt to those who accepted the identification
of Succoth with Theku in the valley (Map 2).

The story of the exodus as given for instance
by Naville, one of the earliest formulators of a
definite route, is as follows: Setting out from
Rameses the Israelites pass the district of Succoth
and reach Etham, a desert region, lying according
to Naville to the west and south of Lake Timsah.
Here they are commanded to turn southward and
encamp before Pi-hahiroth, between Migdol and
the sea, over against Baal-zephon.   Naville identifies all these three places.   Pi-hahiroth is for him
Pi-keheret, House of Keheret the Snake Goddess,
a place mentioned on the famous Pithom stela,
inscribed by King Ptolemy Philadelphos, who
came to the throne in 285 B.C., and he identifies it
with the later town of Serapiu, on the west edge of
the present southern extension of Lake Timsah.
Migdol he places about three miles south of this,
near the modern railway station called Serapeum,
where there is a mound with ruins of the Persian
period.   East of the camp lies the Red Sea, which,
he believes, in those days extended far more to the
north than it now does, passing through what is
now Lake Timsah up into the Wadi Tumilat and
reaching Heroonpolis.   On the far side of this
gulf the Israelites can see Baal-zephon, which
Naville identifies with a hill which now holds
the tomb of a famous Mohammedan sheikh.

There are innumerable difficulties about such a theory as this. In the first place it assumes wrongly that Rameses is in the Wadi Tumilat and that the exodus started from there. In the second place it accepts the Greek Septuagint translation " Red Sea " instead of the original Hebrew " Sea of Reeds," a substitution made by the Greek translators doubtless precisely because they had made the same mistake of identifying the starting point of the exodus with the Wadi Tumilat. In the third place the identification of Pi-hahiroth with Pi-keheret is philologically impossible[1], and even if it were correct we have no evidence for fixing the site of the town at Serapiu. And finally Naville's identifications of the site of Migdol and Baal-zephon are pure guesswork.

Any attempt to deal scientifically with the question must recognize three points. Firstly, the itinerary given in the Bible is due entirely to

---

[1] Naville defends such loose identifications as this by the statement that names taken over from one language to another are only reproduced approximately without any consultation of "philology and its code of laws." He forgets that philology's "code of laws" is not the mere abstract construction of philologists, but an induction from the concrete facts. Nowhere are these facts better illustrated than in the borrowing of names from Egyptian into Semitic and *vice versa*, the original pronunciation being most accurately and consistently indicated. Thus, in the case of *Keheret* the *Ḳ* could in Hebrew appear only as *ḳ* and not as *ḥ*; moreover, the final *t* of the feminine was almost certainly mute in Egyptian, and therefore in an etymology such as Naville postulates would not have been reproduced by *th* in Hebrew.

document P, compiled at least 800 years after the
exodus, and even if we can fix this itinerary
it will give us not necessarily the route actually
taken by the Israelites but merely the route
ascribed to them by a tradition which has only
come down to us in a very late form.   Secondly,
in the Hebrew version there is no mention of
the Red Sea at all, the expression used in Ex. 14
being simply " the sea," while in 13.18 and 15.4
and 22 it is the " Sea of Reeds," and the translation " Red Sea " being based purely on the fact
that the Greek version uses this.   Thirdly,
Gardiner's work has shown that Rameses-Raamses
is almost beyond doubt Pi-Ramessu, "House of
Rameses," the capital of XIXth Dynasty Egypt,
lying on the site of the later Pelusium.   Once
these facts are grasped it will be realized that the
scene of the exodus in the mind of the compilers
of the biblical narrative is not the Wadi Tumilat,
but a region considerably further to the north.[1]

This is corroborated by the very remarkable
statement (Ex. 13.17) that " God led them not
through the way of the Philistines, although that

---

[1] Sir William Willcocks, in his *From the Garden of Eden to the Crossing
of the Jordan*, p.69, has rightly pointed out that the story of the quails shows
that a northerly route was in the mind of the compiler of the narrative.
These birds drop in thousands on the Mediterranean shore between Egypt
and Palestine, exhausted with their long flight across the sea.   Similar
conditions are not found anywhere on the Gulf of Suez or the Red Sea proper.

was near ; for God said, ' Lest peradventure the
people repent when they see war, and they
return to Egypt.' But God led the people
about by the way of the wilderness of the Sea of
Reeds." There can be no doubt that by " the
way of the Philistines " the writer meant the
great military route which formed the highway,
in ancient as in modern times, from Egypt to
Syria, leaving Egypt at Thel, east of the modern
el-Kantareh, moving slightly north of east along
the southern edge of Lake Serbonis, reaching
the sea at el-'Arish, and passing through Rafa to
Gaza. A glance at Map 2 will convince the
reader that, while for a people leaving Egypt
by the Wadi Tumilat this road could not possibly
be described as " near," yet for a people moving
out from Pelusium (Rameses) it is so near and
so obviously the route to take that the compiler
is but doing his duty in explaining why it was
not taken.

There is an alternative to the first or Egyptian
portion of this military road, namely the track
leading by the sea over the narrow spit of land
which separates Lake Serbonis from the Mediterranean. This is a much less popular route
than the more southerly one just described,
which it joins eventually before reaching el-'Arish,

though it has on occasion been used for the
transport of troops.   Its unpopularity is doubtless due to its exposed nature, to the prevalence
of quicksands, and to its liability to sudden
swamping through a north wind. Some, however, have identified it with the route of the
exodus, and it obviously furnishes a simple
explanation of the overwhelming of Pharaoh
and his Egyptians.

Assuming then a start from Pelusium, can we
identify more of the biblical place names ?   The
first stage is Succoth, for which no identification
has been proposed except Theku, in the Wadi
Tumilat. Philologically, as was seen in the
previous chapter, the identification is not happy,
and now that we have disengaged ourselves from
the idea of an exodus by this route it may be
given up without regret. The next stage is
Etham which is " in the edge of the wilderness."
This again has not been satisfactorily identified.
It has been suggested that it stands for the
Egyptian word *khetem* " a fortress " and is an
abbreviation of " The fortress of Thel," but, in
addition to the fact that the Egyptian *kh* would
hardly be rendered in Hebrew by *aleph*, there
is no authority for the use of " The Fortress "
alone for Thel.   However this may be, we are

already faced with a difficulty, for the Israelites, despite their having marched two whole stages from Pelusium, have only just reached the " edge of the wilderness." But for the moment let us proceed. They now " turn and encamp before Pi-hahiroth, between Migdol and the sea, over against Baal-zephon : before it shall ye encamp by the sea. For Pharaoh will say of the children of Israel, ' They are entangled in the land, the wilderness hath shut them in.' " It would seem from this that the turn made by the wanderers is of the nature of a return into Egypt, and, moreover, it brings them to " the sea." How do the place-names agree with this. Pi-hahiroth is unknown. Baal-zephon is also unknown, though on the verso of the papyrus Sallier IV is mentioned a goddess called Baalit-zephon. Bearing a Semitic name, the place should lie on the extreme edge of Egyptian territory, perhaps actually in Bedawi country, and its signification " Baal of the North " is undoubtedly a confirmation of the northerly locality of the scene of the exodus. With regard to Migdol there is more to be said. Migdol is simply the Semitic word for a tower ; but it was borrowed by the Egyptians, probably as early as the XVIIIth Dynasty, and became a very popular name for towns. A Cairo papyrus mentions no fewer than four Migdols in the Eastern Delta alone, but it is worthy of note that only one of these is called Migdol simply, without further qualification. This one may well be identical with the Magdolo of the Antonine Itinerary, described as lying half-way between Pelusium and Sele (Thel), at a distance of 12 Roman miles from each. An important town called Migdol was known to the Hebrew prophets, and that it was situated in the extreme north-east corner of the Delta would seem clear from the passages in which Ezekiel (29.10, and 30.6 marginal rendering in Authorised Version) curses Egypt " from Migdol to Syene," where Syene is the modern Aswan at the First Cataract, the southern extremity of Egypt, and Migdol must stand for the northern. Jeremiah, too, speaks of Migdol together with Daphnae and Memphis (44.1 and 46.14). We are probably justified in concluding that in late Egyptian days there was a town called Migdol, in the north-eastern Delta, which was of considerable size and importance, and since on other grounds we have found the scene of the exodus to lie in this part of Egypt, it is not unlikely that this town was in the mind of the compiler of the exodus narrative. The site of

this Migdol has been with great probability
identified with the mound called Tell el-Her,
which does indeed lie roughly half-way between
Pelusium and Thel, and which seems the only
likely site in the neighbourhood. It lies a little
to the north of the great military road, but it
is probably, despite this, identical with the
Migdol of Menmare (King Seti I) shown in the
Karnak sculptures illustrating the Asiatic campaigns of Seti I of the XIXth Dynasty.

One passage, however, at first sight seems to
point to a Migdol of Seti I as lying near Theku,
a district in the Wadi Tumilat, and therefore
to tell against a northern localization of the
exodus. In the papyrus Anastasi V, 19.6 to 20.2,
a difficult and probably corrupt passage, we read
in the report of an officer sent to recover some
escaped slaves, " I was despatched from the
Courts of the Royal Palace on the ninth day of
the third month of summer, at eventide, in quest
of those two servants. I reached the enclosure
wall of Theku (probably Tell el-Maskhuteh) on
the tenth day of the third month of summer,
where they told me that they had said in the
south that they (the slaves) had passed on the
tenth (sic ?) day of the third month of summer.
And when I reached the fortress they told me

that the groom had come from the desert to say
that they had passed the north wall of the
Migdol of Seti-Merneptah (Seti I)." It is
impossible to discern exactly what is happening
in this passage, one thing alone is certain, namely
that it contains nothing to contradict the identification of this Migdol with Tell el-Her.
Gardiner is right in pointing out that it was only
the incorrect identification of Theku with
Succoth and the desire to "co-ordinate this
passage with the story of the exodus" that gave
rise to the belief that the Migdol of Seti I here
mentioned was other than the well-known
Migdol of Seti I, probably at Tell el-Her.

Summing up the evidence it may be said that
we have considerable reason for believing that by
Migdol the compiler of the narrative intended
the Migdol of Seti I, lying half-way between
Pelusium and Thel. Yet in the absence of any
indication of the positions of Baal-zephon and
Pi-hahiroth it would be the merest waste of time
to try to reconstruct the route which lay in the
mind of the compiler. All we can be sure about
is that it is to be looked for not in the Wadi
Tumilat but much further to the north, in the
region of Pelusium and Tell el-Her.

In this case what is the Sea of Reeds which

figures so prominently in the story? Clearly it is not the Red Sea, as the Greek translators thought, but some piece of water on the edge of the Mediterranean fresh enough to allow reeds to grow in it.[1] The continual changes which take place in the extension and nature of the lagoons which edge the sea between Egypt and Palestine make it almost a waste of time to attempt to place more closely the position of the biblical " Sea of Reeds." The result would also depend very largely on the exact amount and kind of credence which we place on the story of the crossing of the Sea of Reeds. Thus, if we believe that a passage was miraculously made for the Israelites it is useless to look for a suitable spot, for it might have happened anywhere. On the other hand, those who believe that the Israelites reaped the advantage of a natural phenomenon so impressive as to appear to them in their circumstances miraculous have met with little success in trying to find a spot where an east wind could have produced the effect attributed to it. Others have concentrated on the incident of the destruction of Pharaoh's charioteers, and

[1] In I Kings 9.26, the Sea of Reeds is quite clearly the Gulf of Akaba, and possibly also in Numb. 21.4. It is obvious that it cannot have that meaning here. For an ingenious suggestion with regard to this point and others concerning the first part of the route of the exodus see a forthcoming article by A. H. Gardiner in *Mélanges Champollion*, Paris, 1922, pp. 231-241.

have looked for a locality where such an event might reasonably have taken place. The varying conclusions to which the searchers after truth in these matters have come only serve to show the inadequacy of the evidence to prove anything whatsoever. Unless some new means be found of identifying more of the geographical names given by Document P we are hardly likely to make much progress towards fixing the scheme of the exodus which existed in the mind of the author of that document, and even then we shall be as uncertain as ever regarding the route actually taken by the emigrants.

K

CHAPTER VI

FROM the time of the exodus, whenever that may have been, the biblical narrative mentions neither Egypt nor the Egyptians until the reign of Solomon ; thus from the point of view of Hebrew-Egyptian relations the period of the judges and the early part of the monarchy is a blank. During these years great changes had taken place in Egypt. It has been seen in Chapter V that the great Egyptian empire of the XVIIIth Dynasty, begun by its earliest kings, the expellers of the Hyksos, and extended to its widest limits by Thothmes III, had fallen to pieces in the reign of Akhenaton (Amenhotp IV), 1375-1350 B.C. This king was followed by his son-in-law Sakere, who after a short reign gave place to another son-in-law Tut-ankh-aton, " Living image of the Disk." The latter, finding popular and probably priestly prejudice too strong for him, relinquished the worship of the Sun's Disk and returned to the orthodox cult of Amon, moving the court back to Thebes and changing his name to Tut-ankh-

amon, " Living image of Amon." It needed
a stronger man, however, to deal with the state
of internal chaos into which Egypt had fallen
during the heresy, and a famous inscription has
preserved to our days the enactments by which
Horemheb restored order and security.

This king is reckoned as the first of the XIXth
Dynasty, and was followed by two conquerors,
Seti I and Ramesses II, who recovered a very
considerable portion of Thothmes' empire in
Palestine and Syria. The recovery, however, was
but short-lived, for the great movements of
peoples which set the Mediterranean in a turmoil
about 1200 B.C. did not leave Egypt unscathed,
and though she managed under Merenptah, the
successor of Ramesses II, and later under Ramesses
III, the first king of the XXth Dynasty, to save
her own shores from all but the most temporary
invasion, she was forced to relinquish her Asiatic
dependencies. From this moment her story is
for many years one of decline. A series of
Pharaohs, each bearing the famous name of
Ramesses, and each unworthy of it, followed one
another, until, under Ramesses XII, the high
priest of Amon at Thebes displaced his king and
seated himself upon the throne, thus founding the
XXIst Dynasty, about 1090 B.C. This priest,

Hrihor by name, was, however, unable to control the whole of Egypt, and a rival, Nesubanebded, succeeded in establishing himself at Tanis as king of the Delta.

The degradation at which Egypt had arrived is well illustrated by the story of Wenamon, an envoy sent by Hrihor to the Syrian coast to procure wood from the Lebanon for the building of the sacred boat of Amon. Arrived at Byblos, with a mere handful of silver to pay for the timber, and an image of Amon which would, it was hoped, secure him a favourable hearing, he is at first ordered by Theker-baal, the Prince of Byblos, to remove himself. An accident, however, causes the prince to revoke this harsh command, but from the manner in which he delays the envoy day by day for eight months, and from the haughty tone in which he addresses him, it is evident that the prestige of Egypt in Syria has gone, and that what had been demanded almost as a right by a Ramesses II must be begged for with humility by a Hrihor.

The end of the XXIst Dynasty with its divided rule may be easily foretold. Once again Egypt paid the inevitable penalty of disunion ; she was invaded from the west by the Libyans, who first established themselves in the Delta, and gradually

extended their rule over the whole of Egypt.
For two centuries, roughly 945 to 745 B.C.,
Libyan kings ruled in the Nile valley, and it is
in this period that the events fall which again
give us our points of contact with Palestine.

After what has been said in Chapter I it will
here be necessary merely to remind the reader
that we are now arriving at a portion of the
biblical story which is historical, not in the sense
that every detail is correct, but in the sense that
the main lines of the story are derived from
contemporary documents.

In I Kings, 11.14-22 we read that "the Lord
stirred up an adversary to Solomon, Hadad the
Edomite : he was of the king's seed in Edom."
This Hadad, a member of the royal family of
Edom, had fled to Egypt as a child, at the time
when David had defeated his country and
"smitten every male in Edom." In Egypt he
was well received by the Pharaoh, whose name is
not mentioned, who gave him in marriage the
sister of Tahpenes, his own wife, and she bore
him a son, Genubath, who was brought up in the
palace among Pharaoh's sons. After the death
of David and his captain of the host Joab, Hadad,
despite Pharaoh's protests, returned to his own
country. Unfortunately, the narrator is merely

interested in telling us how Solomon was punished for his sins by the raising up of various " advers- aries " and gives us little detail of their deeds; in fact, with regard to the sequel of Hadad's return, we only gather from verse 25 that " he did mischief."

It is, however, relevant to ask what part the Pharaoh was playing in this drama. It is curious that another of Solomon's " adversaries," Jeroboam, also fled into Egypt, and one is tempted to wonder whether the two stories are not doubles of a single event. The detail with which Hadad's story is told is, however, distinctly against such a supposition, and it seems best to take the story at its face value. Since Hadad was already married when David died in 970 B.C. (for the date see p. 112), and was but a child when he fled before David, he must have reached Egypt towards the end of the XXIst Dynasty, possibly in the reign of one of the two last kings of the dynasty, Siamon and Pisebkhanu II. It is, perhaps, scarcely worth while to ask why these rulers at Tanis should give so warm a welcome to the fugitive. We need hardly doubt that the object was political. Possibly the successful and warlike career of David and the conquest by the Israelites of the Philistines had alarmed the Egyptians, who, by kind treatment of Hadad, sought to secure the friendship of his country and to use Edom as a buffer state between themselves and Palestine.

With the accession of Solomon we reach a period of alliance between Egypt and Palestine, for in I Kings 3.1 we are told that " Solomon made affinity with Pharaoh, king of Egypt, and took Pharaoh's daughter, and brought her into the city of David." This is not the first instance of intermarriage between royal houses of Egypt and Asia, the policy having already been inaugurated under the XVIIIth Dynasty, when Amenhotp III, as we know from the Tell el-Amarna letters, received in marriage a daughter of the king of Babylonia and also a daughter of the king of Mitanni. Moreover, Ramesses II married the eldest daughter of a Hittite ruler.

The name of the Egyptian king to whom Solomon became a son-in-law is not recorded, but we can arrive at it with a considerable degree of probability. The new queen was lodged in the city of David until Solomon should have "made an end of building his own house, and the house of the Lord." The temple was begun in his fourth year (I Kings 6.1), and finished in his eleventh (I Kings 6.37). The building of his own house

occupied 13 years (I Kings 7.1), and from 9.20
it is clear that it followed at once on the completion of the temple, for the two together
occupied him twenty years. The marriage therefore took place some time between his accession
about 970 B.C. and his 24th year, 945 B.C. This
latter date is in Egypt the generally accepted
year for the beginning of the reign of Sheshonk I,
the first king of the XXIInd or Libyan Dynasty,
and, could this dating be regarded as certain, it
would be probable that Solomon's wife was the
daughter of one of the last kings of the XXIst or
Tanite Dynasty, perhaps of Siamon or Pisebkhanu
II. Unfortunately the Egyptian dates are
nothing more than approximate, and Sheshonk
may well have come to the throne several years
earlier than 945 B.C., in which case the princess
whom Solomon married might quite well be his
daughter.

There is perhaps one argument in favour of
such a supposition. Almost more interesting
than the alliance itself is the wedding gift which
the king of Egypt gave to his daughter. " For
Pharaoh king of Egypt had gone up and taken
Gezer, and burnt it with fire, and slain the
Canaanites that dwelt in the city, and given it
for a present to his daughter, Solomon's wife."

This must have been a peculiarly pleasing gift, for Gezer was precisely one of those towns from which the Israelites had never succeeded in dislodging the Canaanites (Judges 1.29). It has been rightly pointed out that the ability of the Egyptian king to sack Gezer assumes his mastery over the Philistine country on the coast, for Gezer commands one of the main routes which leads up from the coastal plain to the hill country of Palestine, which the Philistines of David's time had been so anxious to win, and that an Egyptian should advance as far north as Gezer without securing his left flank is unthinkable (Map 1). In Egypt this campaign, extensive as it must have been, has left no certain trace. Its political significance is however clear. The Egyptians are once more attracted by the hope of empire in Syria-Palestine. The first step is an alliance by marriage with Solomon, king of the Israelites, accompanied by an attack on the Philistine plain. Solomon, to whom this last might seem a matter for anxiety, is propitiated by the gift of Gezer, which would enable him to secure his land against possible aggression by the Philistines, still a redoubtable foe. The following up of this new policy in Syria-Palestine is not long delayed, and as soon as Solomon is removed by death the

Egyptians, having secured their left flank in the coastal plain, invade both Israel and Judah (see below).

It is a little difficult to reconcile an extensive invasion of the Philistine country and the inauguration of a forward policy in Asia with what we at present know of these feeble kings at the end of the XXIst Dynasty, and it is tempting to attribute the capture of Gezer to the great Sheshonk (Shishak) himself. Is this possible chronologically? We have just seen that the absolute date of Sheshonk's accession is too rough to help us. We can, however, establish a relative dating, for we know that Shishak invaded Rehoboam in the latter's fifth year. According to the biblical chronology of Kings, Solomon reigned forty years (a figure which, it is true, is in itself suspect), and married the daughter of the conqueror of Gezer not later than his twenty-fourth year, possibly not later than his eleventh, for I Kings 3.1 gives the impression that the temple was not completed at the time. The space between this marriage and the capture of Jerusalem is at least twenty-one years, and possibly even thirty-four years. Of Shishak we only know with certainty that he reigned at least twenty-one years, and there is a slight presump-

tion (see below) that the expedition into Israel
and Judah took place not long before his twenty-
first year. It is thus within the bounds of
possibility that he was the despoiler of Gezer and
the father of Solomon's wife, a possibility which
must not be ruled out by the change of policy
towards Palestine involved by the invasion under
Rehoboam. The question cannot, however, be
decided until fresh evidence enables us to fix the
true length and details of Solomon's reign and the
exact date and length of Shishak's.

Before leaving Solomon's reign we have still to
consider the difficult passages which refer to his
obtaining horses out of Egypt. In I Kings 10.28
we read in the Authorized Version that " Solomon
had horses brought out of Egypt, and linen yarn :
the king's merchants received the linen yarn at
a price." Now the Hebrew text of this passage is
manifestly corrupt; but, if anything is certain
about it, it is that the words "linen yarn" never
stood there at all. By a slight change in the
pointing (*i.e.*, in the vocalization, which was not
indicated in the old Hebrew, but added by much
later scribes), and the addition of the word "and,"
which in Hebrew is a mere stroke, we can get a
perfectly intelligible translation : " Solomon had
horses brought out of Mizraim and out of Kue ;

the king's merchants received them out of Kue
at a price." The correctness of this rendering is,
perhaps, supported by the Greek version of the
Septuagint, which appears to read, though not
quite grammatically, "The going forth of
Solomon's horsemen was out of Egypt, and the
king's merchants were out of Thekoue ; and they
received (them) out of Thekoue by barter."
Here it has been suggested that Thekoue is a
combination of the Egyptian word for "land" with
Kue, so that Thekoue would stand for "the land
of Kue." Now it is clear from the Assyrian texts
that this land lay in Cilicia (Map 1). Moreover,
on the obelisk of Shalmaneser II recording the
battle of Qarqar the countries of Kue and Musri
are closely juxtaposed, and might thus be expected
to lie close together. It has therefore been
suggested that in the passage we are considering,
the Hebrew Mizraim, which elsewhere in the Old
Testament certainly means Egypt, stands for the
country of Musri which lay in Cilicia or Northern
Syria. This suggestion is accepted by those who
find a difficulty in supposing an export of horses
from Egypt, where indeed the horse was known at
this time, but where the evidence for its being
bred for export is rather scanty.[1] They point

[1] See, however, the remarkable passage Deut. 17.16 (below, p. 192).

with justice to the well-known fact that in ancient times Cilicia was famous for its horses. To this others have replied that in the Assyrian inscriptions of this period the word Musri can quite reasonably be taken as referring in every case to Egypt and not to the Cilician Musri; this latter is, it is true, mentioned in Assyrian inscriptions, but only in those dating from the last few centuries of the second millenium B.C. They see no inherent improbability in the exportation of horses from Egypt, or in the supposition that Solomon procured his horses from two entirely separate countries, Egypt and Kue.

It would be hard indeed to say on which side the balance of probability lies. Seeing that the Hebrew text is hopelessly corrupt, and that the Greek version, though suggesting a reasonable emendation, is far from inspiring confidence, it is barely worth while to devote much time or space to theories based on such uncertain foundations.

The next events in the relations of Israel and Egypt mark an important moment in the biblical narrative, which for the first time records the name of an Egyptian king, and fortunately one

which can be identified. The biblical Shishak
is beyond all question the first ruler of the Libyan
XXIInd Dynasty, Sheshonk I. His name first
occurs in I Kings 11.40, where he welcomes in
Egypt the fugitive Jeroboam, the son of Nebat,
who was one of the " adversaries " whom God
raised up against Solomon. The close parallel
offered by this story to that of Hadad has already
been remarked. Politically it would appear to
mean that the friendly relations with Solomon
marked by the royal alliance were coming to an
end, and that Egypt, having possibly already
subdued the Philistine country, was now only
waiting for a suitable opportunity for interfering
in the hill country of Palestine. The opportunity
came with the death of Solomon, followed by the
return of Jeroboam to Palestine, perhaps sent
thither by Shishak with the direct intention of
causing division and weakness, and by the split
of the kingdom into Judah and Israel. Whether
Shishak consciously engineered this scission or not
he made no delay in taking advantage of it, for
the biblical story tells us that " it came to pass,
in the fifth year of king Rehoboam, that Shishak
king of Egypt came up against Jerusalem : And
he took away the treasures of the house of the
Lord, and the treasures of the king's house ; he

even took away all." (I Kings 14.25-26). The account in II Chron. 12.2 gives a little more detail; " With twelve hundred chariots, and threescore thousand horsemen : and the people were without number which came with him out of Egypt ; the Lubims, the Sukiims, and the Ethiopians. And he took the fenced cities which pertained to Judah, and came to Jerusalem." That the numbers quoted are valueless is clear from the fact that the Egyptians never fought on horseback, but only in chariots, two men to each chariot, so that twelve hundred chariots implies only 2,400 " horsemen," while 60,000 horsemen would require 30,000 chariots. The Lubims are the Libyans, who doubtless under Shishak formed the chief portion of the Egyptian army. The Kushim are the inhabitants of Kush or Upper Nubia (Ethiopia). No reasonable suggestion has yet been made for the identification of the Sukiims, rendered in the Septuagint by Trogodutai, probably meant for Troglodutai or " Cave-dwellers."

In the biblical account the invasion appears as affecting only Judah. This is merely due to the fact that the narrative in which it appears is one which keeps apart the story of the two kingdoms, except when narrating relations between the two, and here it is dealing with Judah alone. That Israel as well as Judah felt the force of Shishak's arm is evident from the Egyptian version of the story, from which it is abundantly clear that the campaign was no interference in Palestine in the interest of his former guest Jeroboam, but a serious attempt at empire-building in Syria. Shisak's main contribution to Egyptian architecture was the building or continuation of the great southern court of the temple of Amon at Karnak. Here, on the wall, near what is now known as the Bubastite Gate, he inscribed the record of his campaign in Palestine. On the right is the figure of the king, never finished, and now almost totally lost, holding by the hair a group of kneeling Syrians and brandishing his club over their heads. On the left the god Amon and certain other deities lead forward 156 captives, each symbolising a Palestinian town or district the name of which is written in an oval completely covering the lower half of each man. Many of the names have perished, and not more than about half are now legible with certainty. Much controversy has gathered round this list, many wishing to regard it as a mere copy of that of some earlier XVIIIth or XIXth Dynasty conqueror. But though such a thing is by no means impossible or unparalleled in Egypt there is not a fragment of evidence that Sheshonk's list is a copy, and the idea has mainly been suggested by the failure to realize that the presence of names of towns in Israel as well as in Judah does not in the least impugn the accuracy of the biblical account, which only deals with Judah (see above). Even some of those who admit the originality of the list have found the presence of these Israel names difficult in view of the biblical limitation of the campaign to Judah, and have endeavoured to explain them as merely places at which the Egyptian army touched in a friendly spirit, or places which gave tribute to the invader and were not attacked. This is a good instance of an unsound procedure. Here we have a list of conquered towns, which in itself is in no way suspect. To throw this evidence over merely because the Bible story does not (and that for a good reason already given) mention an invasion of Israel, is merely to reject positive evidence for negative. To raise the difficulty that Shishak would hardly have attacked his former guest in this way is to display complete ignorance of Egyptian, and indeed of all Eastern diplomacy.

The list itself is not without interest. The larger towns mentioned are all in Israel, though

L

none lie north of the Kishon valley. Judah, on
the other hand, is represented by small and
mostly unidentifiable places, but it is highly
probable that the larger towns, including
Jerusalem itself, stood in ovals which are now
destroyed. Among the more interesting names
are Yadhamelek and "The Field of Abram."
The first of these was by early philologists read
Judah-melek and translated " the king of Judah " ;
the absurdity of this has long been recognized,
and the error is now perpetuated only by the
Luxor dragomans, who point out the captive
bearing this town-name as Rehoboam, in the
hope of an extra five piastres from the pious
tourist. The " Field of Abram " merely shows
the survival of this name, not necessarily that of
the patriarch, in a place-name in Palestine.

Unfortunately for our chronological researches
Shishak did not record the year of his reign in
which this campaign took place, or, if he did, it
has perished. We have, however, a rock inscription in the sandstone quarries of Gebel Silsileh
in which the architect Horemsaf relates how he
had been entrusted with the quarrying of stone
for the work which his master Shishak intended
to carry out in the temple of Amon at Karnak.
This inscription is dated in the 21st year of the

reign, and there is a strong possibility that the
Palestine campaign had already taken place,
though we must not ignore the possibility that
the war inscription, which bears no date, is later
than the actual building to which reference is
here made. Should this be the case it would
the more easily enable us to equate Shishak with
the conqueror of Gezer and father of Solomon's
wife (see above, p. 154). It is even possible that
an inscription of Shishak found on a stela at
Karnak, which speaks of a victory on the shores
of Kemwer, a lake on the isthmus of Suez, records
the beginnings of the campaign against the
Philistines and Gezer.

No more is heard of Egypt in the biblical
narrative until we come to the difficult question
of the invasion of Judah in the reign of Asa by
Zerah the Ethiopian (II Chron. 14. 9-15). The
date of this from the Palestinian side is easily
fixed. Rehoboam ruled seventeen years ; his
successor Abijah three years. The latter was
followed by Asa, under whom "the land was quiet
ten years" (II Chron. 14.1). The invasion of
Zerah must therefore fall after this, that is to
say at least 25 years later than Shishak's capture
of Jerusalem in the fifth year of Rehoboam.

Moreover it seems a legitimate inference from
II Chron. 15.10, taken with its context, that
Asa's victory actually took place in his fifteenth
year or just before, that is thirty years after the
capture of Jerusalem. In Egypt this would bring
us almost certainly into the reign of Osorkon I,
the successor of Shishak, a king who ruled
thirty-six years. The slight similarity of the
names Zerah (Greek Zare) and Osorkon has
tempted many to identify them and to regard
the incident as a fresh attempt on the part of
Egypt to reconquer the whole of Palestine. But
there are difficulties. Philologically it is absolutely impossible to get Zerah out of Osorkon,
though many ingenious attempts have been
made. Thus if these two names are one and the
same the Hebrew form has been so transformed
that it is no longer recognizable. On the other
hand it is noteworthy that Zerah's army, after
its defeat by Asa at Mareshah in the valley of
Zephathah, was pursued to Gerar, which is held
by some to indicate that it was making for Egypt
by the shortest route in its flight. Yet it is
difficult to see how, during the reign of Osorkon
the Libyan, or indeed during the early part of
the dynasty to which he belonged, an Ethiopian
could be in a position to lead an army against

Palestine. It is true that in II Chron. 16.8 Libyans are said to have taken part in this campaign as well as Ethiopians, but this is probably an error which has crept through a false analogy with II Chron. 12.3.

In view of these serious difficulties two explanations of the incident have been proposed. Firstly that the whole story is an invention by a patriotic Hebrew writer anxious to balance Shishak's humiliation of Judah by a subsequent victory of Asa over the Egyptians, and secondly that the Hebrew Kushim, translated here "Ethiopians," in reality refers to a people of this name living in Arabia. The first explanation is perhaps too radical. The second, although it might be urged in its defence that " tents of cattle " and " sheep and camels in abundance " are a booty more likely to be taken from an Arabian tribe than from an Egyptian army (the camel not being in use in Egypt at this date), is based on the hypothesis of a Kush in Arabia which has yet to be proved.

The whole incident in fact is difficult on present evidence. The Ethiopian conquest of Egypt did not take place until 150 years after these events. On the other hand, the vicissitudes of Egypt in the first millennium B.C. were such that a Hebrew writer might well be excused for having very hazy ideas as to the nationality of its kings at any particular moment, and might well have written Zerah the Ethiopian for Zerah the Libyan. There would still remain the difficulty that we have no Libyan king bearing this name.

At the same time it is hard to rid oneself of the impression that the story records, if inaccurately, some new collision with Egypt. Why else does Asa smite the cities around Gerar ? This part of Palestine must surely have fallen into Egyptian hands after the campaign of Gezer and that which ended in the fall of Jerusalem. Zerah, defeated at Mareshah, retires on Gerar, which, with the towns in its neighbourhood, has an Egyptian garrison. The victorious Asa pursues him and expels the garrisons from Gerar and its district. It is difficult to see in this anything but a fresh and unsuccessful attack by Egypt on Palestine. On the Egyptian side there is nothing against it, but if we do accept it let us be perfectly clear that the supposed equation of the names Zerah and Osorkon is far too uncertain to be urged in its support.

CHAPTER VII

SO AND TIRHAKAH

WE now enter on an entirely new phase in the relations of Palestine and Egypt. The change is due to the expansion towards the west of the second Assyrian Empire. A glance at the map will show that Syria and Palestine form the natural way of communication between Assyria and Egypt, the more direct route being impracticable by reason of its desert nature. The consequence of this was that as soon as Assyria, as well as Egypt, began to cherish designs of empire in Syria-Palestine the petty kingdoms of this country were bound to serve as buffer states between their two powerful neighbours, vassals now of the one and now of the other, occasionally for short intervals free from allegiance to either.

The rise of the second Assyrian Empire may be dated to the reign of Adad-nirari II, who reigned from 911 to 890 B.C. In this reign, incidentally, begins the series of lists of eponymous magistracies which enables us to date to the exact year the main events of Assyrian history. Ashur-nasir-pal III, who reigned from 884 to 860, was the first monarch of this period to come into direct contact with Syria, for he overran the Lebanon and reached Phoenicia and the sea. At his death the Aramaean kingdoms of Hamath and Damascus revolted, and at the great battle of Qarqar in 854 B.C., we find Ahab of Israel in alliance with Benhadad II (Hadad-idri) of Damascus, and Irkhuleni of Hamath, against the might of Assyria. Shalmaneser II, the Assyrian king, records the battle as a victory, but since Benhadad II remained in possession of his kingdom this is doubtless an exaggeration. Amongst the allies on the Israelite side appear 1,000 men of Musri, in whom some see Egyptians, while others would assume them to be from the Musri in Northern Syria or Cilicia.

If we set aside this rather doubtful piece of evidence the first actual contact between Assyria and Egypt does not occur until a century later. In 734 B.C. the Assyrian Tiglath-pileser IV entered Syria, and marching south into the country of the Philistines captured Gaza, thus bringing the Assyrian arms within striking distance of Egypt (Map 1). Meanwhile, in Egypt itself, great changes had taken place. The Libyans of the XXIInd Dynasty had ruled for two centuries, from about 945 to 745 B.C. The first three kings of the XXIIIrd Dynasty were also Libyans, but their power was undoubtedly waning, and in the reign of the second of these, Osorkon III, Egypt was invaded by a certain Piankhi, king of the Ethiopian kingdom which had its capital at Napata, far up the Nile. Recent excavations have shown that these Ethiopian kings were themselves of Libyan descent. After a victorious campaign in Egypt Piankhi withdrew to Napata as suddenly as he had come, and left Osorkon III ruling at Thebes, side by side with a number of other petty dynasts in the Delta. These between them constitute the XXIIIrd and XXIVth Dynasties. About 712 B.C. the Ethiopians again attacked Egypt and one of them, Shabaka, brother of Piankhi, assumed the throne as first ruler of the XXVth or Ethiopian Dynasty.

It is at this critical moment in the history of Egypt that the Old Testament gives us our next point of contact between Egypt and Palestine. We find in II Kings 17.1 ff. that Hoshea reigned in Samaria over Israel nine years. " Against him came up Shalmaneser king of Assyria; and Hoshea became his servant, and gave him presents. And the king of Assyria found conspiracy in Hoshea :

for he had sent messengers to So king of Egypt (Mizraim), and brought no present to the king of Assyria, as he had done year by year; therefore the king of Assyria shut him up and bound him in prison. Then the king of Assyria came up throughout all the land, and went up to Samaria, and besieged it three years. In the ninth year of Hoshea the king of Assyria took Samaria, and carried Israel away into Assyria." This is a perfectly clear account. Hoshea is tributary to Assyria. So or Seve the king of Egypt intrigues with him and persuades him to withhold his yearly tribute, with consequences disastrous for Samaria. But who is So, king of Egypt? The name rendered So in our translation, and Soa by most manuscripts of the Greek version, was probably pronounced something like Sev'e or even Seb'e, and it is practically certain that the same person is referred to by Shalmaneser's successor Sargon in his Annals for 720 B.C., where " Sib'i, the *turtan* (commander-in-chief) of Musri " is mentioned as among those defeated at the battle of Raphia. Just as So was the ally of the revolting Hoshea in 726, so here in 720 Sib'i is in league with the rebel Hanum of Gaza, and in view of the close similarity of the names, the phonetic correspondence of which is beyond reproach, it is

highly probable that they are to be regarded as
one and the same. The fact that in the one case
he is called "king" and in the other "commander-
in-chief" need cause no misgiving, for in the
period in question it would probably be difficult
even for an Egyptian to decide who was actually
"king of Egypt." The main result of these
intrigues so far as Egypt is concerned was that
in 715 B.C. we find Pir'u the king of Musri, *i.e.*
Pharaoh, king of Egypt, mentioned among a list
of rulers who rendered tribute to Assyria.

Some authorities have attempted to identify
this So or Sib'i with Shabaka, the Ethiopian king
of Egypt. On philological grounds this is quite
impossible, for the *aleph* (which is here rendered ')
of the Hebrew and Assyrian forms cannot possibly
stand for the Egyptian or Ethiopian *k* of Shabaka
or Sabaka. Brugsch did indeed suggest that the
-*ka* was merely the definite article, as in modern
Nubian, and, since *sab* in the same language
means a wild cat, he proposed to translate the
name as "the wild cat," and suggested that in
the Hebrew form Seb'e the definite article had
been omitted. But it has been pointed out
that the modern Barabra speech of Nubia was
not necessarily the speech of the Ethiopian kings,
and that Brugsch's -*ka* (more correctly -*ki*) is

not the definite article but a case-ending. More-over, the Egyptian Shabaka is in the Annals of Ashurbanipal rendered in Assyrian by Shabaku, and can therefore hardly be identical with Sib'i.

Even if philology could admit the identity of Seb'e and Shabaka there would still remain serious chronological difficulties, for the fall of Samaria is dated by Assyrian sources to 722 B.C., and So's intrigue must therefore have occurred not later than 725 B.C., whereas Shabaka, according to Egyptian dating, did not come to the throne of Egypt until about 712 B.C. Unless, therefore, we suppose some serious error in the accepted Egyptian dating for the accession of Shabaka we must not attempt to identify him with So. Hall, who accepts the equation Shabaka equals Seve or So, avoids the difficulty by supposing that when Piankhi conquered Egypt about 727 B.C. he left his brother Shabaka as commander in Egypt while he himself retired to Napata. This, however, is a pure guess, and is supported by nothing in the Egyptian inscriptions.

Putting aside the fanciful and now discredited belief of Winckler that by Mizraim in this passage (as in many others) is meant not Egypt but a hypothetical land of Musri somewhere in Arabia, the wisest course would seem to be to identify So

king of Egypt with one of those numerous petty
dynasts who ruled in the Egyptian Delta during
the years which elapsed between Piankhi's conquest of Egypt and Shabaka's establishing himself
on the Egyptian throne.

Shortly afterwards an Egyptian king was
tempted to interfere once more in Palestinian
politics. In 715 B.C. Ashdod and other towns
revolted against Assyria under the instigation
of a man whose proper name or, perhaps, whose
ethnic name was Yamani. Sargon tells us that
they sent gifts to Pir'u, king of Musri, " a prince
who could not help them, and asked him for an
alliance." Whether the alliance was granted or
not we do not gather. The rebellion was crushed
—Isaiah 20.1 mentions the fall of Ashdod—and
Yamani fled " to the land of Musri, which belongs
to the territory of Melukhkha," where the king of
Melukhkha put him in irons and sent him to
Assyria. The identification of Melukhkha in
this passage is a very thorny problem which
cannot here be discussed at length. The balance
of probability appears to lie with the view that
in certain Assyrian inscriptions of this period the
term was used in an archaistic sense instead of the
more usual Kushi to represent Ethiopia. The

very curious description of Musri as dependent (politically, no doubt, rather than merely geo-graphically) on Melukhkha, difficult to account for on any other hypothesis, is now easily explained as due to the fact that Egypt had just come under the domination of Ethiopia. Yamani's flight must have taken place in 711 B.C., when, according to Egyptian dating, Shabaka the Ethiopian had just conquered Egypt. The gifts of Ashdod had been sent presumably not to him but to one of the feeble monarchs who preceded him in Egypt Proper (Musri), whom he had possibly in the meantime deposed. His surrender of the fugitive was doubtless meant as a show of friendship towards Assyria. Confirmation of this friendly attitude is seen by some in the discovery at Nineveh of a clay sealing of Shabaka which had originally served to close some package sent from the king of Egypt to Assyria.

The accession to the Assyrian throne of Sennacherib in 705 B.C. marks a new stage in the relations of Egypt and Palestine. The death of Sargon had led both in east and west to extensive revolts against Assyrian supremacy, and for the first few years of his reign Sennacherib was fully occupied in crushing the rebels in the immediate vicinity of Assyria. Meantime the Philistines were in open mutiny, and they had been joined by Hezekiah of Judah. What followed we know both from II Kings 18 and 19 and from Sennacherib's own account, inscribed on the so-called Taylor Prism. The biblical account presents certain complications and difficulties which, as they do not affect the Egyptian share in the campaign, may be passed over. From the prism it is clear that Sennacherib passed by the hill country of Judah and marched straight into Philistia, where a great battle was fought at Altaqu. In this battle Sennacherib tells us that the Philistines had summoned to their aid the kings of Musri and the troops of the king of Melukhkha. Melukhkha is here certainly Ethiopia, and in the kings of Musri we must see the local dynasts of the Egyptian Delta, who are presumably still enjoying some measure of independence under the suzerainty of the Ethiopian. The date of the battle was 701 B.C.

Now in II Kings 19.9 we find the name of the Ethiopian king given as Tirhakah, and since Tirhakah did not come to the throne until 688 B.C. according to the Egyptian dating, on which considerable confidence may be placed at this point, there is a discrepancy of thirteen years

at least to be accounted for. Two means of
accounting for it have been suggested. The
first is to suppose that Tirhakah did actually
command the Egyptian forces at Altaqu, but
that he was not yet king at the time. An inscription found at Tanis in the Egyptian Delta seems
to suggest that Tirhakah was in the Delta for
some years before his accession to the throne,
and that he occupied a position of some importance there. It is, therefore, not impossible that
the reigning king, Shabaka, put him in command
of the Egyptian troops sent to support the
Philistine and Judaic rising, which indeed had
not improbably been fomented, if not instigated,
by Shabaka himself. That the Hebrew chronicler should call him king in place of commander-
in-chief is not difficult to believe.

The other explanation of the difficulty is to
suppose that the coming of Tirhakah and his
troops, together with the story of the pestilence
which destroyed Sennacherib's army, are
" doubles " of events which in reality belong to
a second campaign of Sennacherib against
Palestine, about 690 B.C. Assyrian sources do
not mention such a campaign, but Herodotus
(II.141) states that Sennacherib marched with a
huge force to attack Egypt, and lay at Pelusium.

Here, however, a vast army of mice devoured the bow-strings and shield-thongs of the Assyrians, so that morning found them an unarmed prey to the Egyptians. It is tempting to see in this some record of the tradition of the plague mentioned in II Kings 19.35.

However these things may be it is clear that the policy of Egypt still consisted in stirring up revolt in Palestine against the Assyrians. Three times had Assyrian armies penetrated Syria to the very boundaries of Egypt, and three times had they, for various reasons, retired without crossing it. But the end could not be long delayed. In 681 B.C. Esarhaddon ascended the Assyrian throne. In 677 he quelled a revolt in Sidon, which there is some reason for believing was instigated by Tirhakah, and the year 675 saw his army actually *en route* for the conquest of Egypt, but recalled by news of peril nearer home. In 670 Tirhakah was foolish enough to incite Tyre to rebellion. Quickly reducing the revolted city, Esarhaddon pressed on against the real authors of the trouble, and for the first time an Assyrian army entered Egyptian territory. Memphis was taken by storm after a hard struggle, and the Delta was seized and garrisoned with Assyrian troops. Tirhakah fled to Thebes,

M

but within a year he had gathered an army, retaken Memphis, and destroyed the foreign garrisons. Esarhaddon, who had returned to Nineveh set out once more for Egypt, but died on the way.

Nevertheless Egypt's hour had sounded, and even the courage and determination of Tirhakah were not enough to avert the final catastrophe. In 668 Ashurbanipal arrived in Egypt with a force which included contingents from his Syrian subjects, and at Karbanit Tirhakah was once more defeated.   Memphis was at once taken, and a Phoenician fleet sailed up the Nile and occupied Thebes.   Tirhakah retired to his Ethiopian home in Napata.

In the next year he was once more in Egypt, intriguing with certain of the local dynasts whom the Assyrians had recognized in the Delta, including Necho of Sais.   The Assyrian garrisons proved too strong for the rebels, and Tirhakah again retired to Nubia, while Necho was sent as a prisoner to Nineveh, where, curious to relate, he was well treated, and from whence he was shortly afterwards sent back to be viceroy of Egypt.   In the last year of Tirhakah's reign, 663 B.C., his successor Tanutamon made a last effort to re-conquer Egypt.   The attempt merely brought down on Egypt the wrath of the Assyrian conqueror. Ashurbanipal states that he appeared in person, quickly recovered the Delta, and sacked Thebes, which had previously been spared. It was to this event that the prophet Nahum referred (3.8-10) when he apostrophized Nineveh in these words " Art thou better than No-Amon (Thebes), that was situate among the rivers, that had the waters round about it, whose rampart was the sea, and her wall was from the sea ?[1] Ethiopia and Egypt were her strength, and it was infinite ; Put and Lubim were thy helpers. Yet she was carried away, she went into captivity : her young children also were dashed in pieces at the top of all the streets ; and they cast lots for her honourable men, and all her great men were bound in chains."

[1] The Hebrew text is in part at least corrupt. Although the word rendered " sea " might equally well mean " the Nile," Spiegelberg finds the passage so unsuitable as a description of Upper Egyptian No-amon, *i.e.* Thebes, that he proposes to refer it to the Lower Egyptian No-amon, which he places at the modern Tell Balamun, in the north-eastern Delta. Of this place we know nothing except the fact that it existed ; it is possible, but surely a little improbable, that the destruction of a town which had made such an impression among foreign nations should have left no trace in Egyptian history.

CHAPTER VIII

THE Assyrian domination of Egypt was not of very long duration. Necho of Sais, established as ruler of that town by the Assyrians, had in all probability been killed in battle by the rebel Tanutamon, and his son Psammetichus, who had thereupon fled to Assyria, was set up by Ashurbanipal in his father's place. This king, founder of the XXVIth Dynasty, proved to be one of the most able rulers ever possessed by Egypt. Seeing that war was imminent between Assyria and Babylon, he took the opportunity to throw off the yoke of the Assyrian governors in Egypt, to suppress his brother dynasts in the Delta, and as early as 654 B.C. he had forced Thebes to acknowledge him. The next few years were devoted to establishing the commercial prosperity of the country. Trade relations with Syria were restored and direct communication opened with several of the Greek states. At the same time a great archaistic revival took place, both in religion and art of every kind. So successfully did the plans of Psammetichus I work out that by 640 B.C. he found himself in a position once more to dispute with Assyria the possession of Syria-Palestine. A distant memory of this campaign is preserved in Herodotus' story that Psammetichus besieged Azotus (Ashdod in Philistia) for twenty-nine years without intermission, until finally he took it. Any success with which the Egyptians met on this expedition was, however, erased by the irruption into Syria of the Scythian hordes.[1]

When in 609 B.C. Psammetichus' son Necho ascended the throne, the time was again ripe for an invasion of Palestine. Assyria, rudely shaken by the Scythian inroad, was now tottering to its fall, and within a year or two the armies of the Medes and the Babylonians were to clamour at its gates. Psammetichus, delaying only to build a fleet, attacked Philistia in his first year. The opening stages of the campaign are undoubtedly alluded to in Jeremiah 47. 1 and 5. " The word of the Lord that came to Jeremiah against the Philistines, before that Pharaoh smote Gaza. . . . Baldness is come upon Gaza ; Askhelon is cut off with the remnant of their valley." The

---

[1] Some, however, hold that these Scythians were actually the defenders of Ashdod against Psammetichus. There is no evidence for this view.

later stages are very briefly touched on by Herodotus II. 159: "He also made war by land upon the Syrians, and defeated them in a pitched battle at Magdolus (probably a garbled form of Megiddo), after which he made himself master of Cadytis (Kadesh?), a large city of Syria." The biblical narrative, however, is much more explicit. In II Kings 23.29 ff. we read that in the days of Josiah king of Judah "Pharaoh-nechoh king of Egypt went up against the king of Assyria to the river Euphrates: and king Josiah went against him; and he slew him at Megiddo when he had seen him." The account of II Chronicles 35.20 ff. is even fuller. Here Necho is said to be on his way "to fight against Carchemish by Euphrates: and Josiah went out against him." The succeeding verses would suggest that Necho was merely seeking a peaceful passage through Judah on his way to challenge Assyria. It is difficult to believe that he should move his army so far afield leaving an unconquered and unreliable neutral in his rear, and the desire of the Egyptian to avoid a conflict and the perversity of Josiah in insisting on it are distinctly puzzling, and should perhaps not be taken too seriously. If Necho pursued his march to the Euphrates on this occasion he failed to provoke

the Assyrians to battle, for it must be clearly
understood that the reference to Carchemish
here made by the Jewish historian has, in reality,
nothing whatever to do with the great battle
fought there a few years later, though he has
quite possibly confused the two campaigns. It
was presumably on his return from the fruitless
march to the Euphrates that Necho deposed
Jehoahaz, the elected successor of Josiah, and
" put him in bands at Riblah, in the land of
Hamath, that he might not reign in Jerusalem ;
and put the land to a tribute of an hundred
talents of silver, and a talent of gold. And
Pharaoh-nechoh made Eliakim the son of Josiah
king in the room of Josiah his father, and turned
his name to Jehoiakim, and took Jehoahaz away :
and he came to Egypt and died there " (II Kings
23.33-34).

The significance of this campaign from the
Egyptian point of view is immense. At a single
stroke Necho had recovered the Egyptian empire
in Asia to its fullest extent, from the borders of
Egypt through Palestine, Syria proper and
Naharina to the upper waters of the Euphrates.
He was, however, not destined to enjoy it long.
In 606 B.C. the combined forces of the Medes
and Babylonians had accomplished the destruction

of Nineveh, and the Assyrian empire was divided between them, the south and south-west falling to Babylon. Nabopolassar, the king of Babylon, was too old to undertake the re-conquest of Syria, but sent his son Nebuchadnezzar in his place. Necho advanced to meet him and was routed in a great battle fought at Carchemish, of which Jeremiah 46.2 has preserved the record. In the ruins of Carchemish has been found a bronze shield which probably belonged to one of the Ionian mercenaries who fought in his army. Pursued by the insults and revilings of Jeremiah and his exultant countrymen (Jeremiah 46) the discomfited army made its way back to Egypt, leaving Syria to fall into the hands of Babylon. " And the king of Egypt came not any more out of his land " we read in II Kings 24.7, " for the king of Babylon had taken from the river of Egypt unto the river Euphrates all that pertained to the king of Egypt." The new masters of Syria-Palestine were not long in making their appearance in Judah, for in 596 B.C. Nebuchad-nezzar captured Jerusalem and deported to Babylon all but the poorest inhabitants of the land (II Kings 24.10 ff.).

The moral effect of this event was so great that during the rest of Necho's reign and during

that of his successor Psammetichus II, 593 to
588 B.C., Egypt abstained from all participation
in Syrian affairs.   Early in the next reign, that
of Apries, the Hebrew Hophra, the policy of
interference was resumed.   In Judah Jehoiakim,
carried off captive by Nebuchadnezzar, had
been followed by his son Jehoiachin, who after
a short reign had also been taken to Babylon.
The successor chosen by the king of Babylon was
Zedekiah, the brother of Jehoiakim.   It is
perhaps not an accident that it was precisely in
the year of Apries' accession that Zedekiah
rebelled against Babylon.   Ezekiel 17.15 records
the fact that Zedekiah " rebelled against him in
sending his ambassadors into Egypt, that they
might give him horses and much people."   The
details of the campaign which followed are
derived solely from the Greek and the Hebrew
historians, and it is difficult to follow the exact
course of events.   Herodotus IV. 161 tells us
that Apries " marched an army to attack Sidon,
and fought a battle with the king of Tyre by
sea," and from Diodorus we gather that he
carried out the subjugation of the whole Phoenician coast.   But we do not know the date of
this expedition, and its relation to the rebellion
of Zedekiah against Babylon is not clear.   It

is, however, not unlikely that it was this movement of Apries which caused the temporary
retreat of Nebuchadnezzar's forces from before
Jerusalem in 587 B.C. (Jeremiah 37.5 and 11).
The relief was but momentary, for in the
following year Jerusalem fell and was destroyed.
Zedekiah was haled before the Assyrian king at
his headquarters at Riblah in northern Syria, and,
after witnessing the slaughter of his sons, was
blinded and carried away to Babylon. Over the
wretched remnant of the people of Judah allowed
to remain in their own land one Gedaliah was
set as governor. This man, after seven months
of rule, was murdered by the adherents of the
old royal house of Judah, and in fear of the
consequences " all the people, both small and
great, and the captains of the armies, arose, and
came to Egypt; for they were afraid of the
Chaldees " (II Kings 25.26). Among these volun-
tary exiles was the prophet Jeremiah, and there
is a cruel irony in the fact that he who for so
long had poured out his execrations upon the
Egyptians and upon the Egyptophile party in
Judah should thus be forced to flee to the country
which he had spent his life in denouncing. The
site chosen for the dwelling place of the exiles
was Tahpanhes, or Daphnae, a town in the Eastern

Delta, which had quite recently come into prominence in Egypt.

Egyptologists are still divided in opinion as to whether the supposed invasion of Egypt by Nebuchadnezzar in 568 B.C. actually took place; the two inscriptions on which the supposition is based are by no means decisive and have certainly been misunderstood by some authorities. There is nothing improbable in such an event, but until further evidence is forthcoming on the point we are not justified in assuming its reality. Jeremiah's " prophecy " (43.9-10) that Nebuchadnezzar would set his throne on the great stones which he (Jeremiah) had hidden in the brick pavement of Pharaoh's house at Daphnae (Tahpanhes) need not necessarily have been fulfilled (*cf.* Ezekiel 29.32). When Petrie excavated the site of Daphnae in the early eighties he found a building begun by Psammetichus I, which he describes as something " more than a mere garrison fortress " and identifies with " Pharaoh's house in Tahpanhes " mentioned by the prophet. In front of this building was found a large brick pavement or platform, which the excavator opines was that in which Jeremiah hid the large stones. It was, unfortunately, much denuded in places, and a search among what remained of it failed to yield the hoped-for stones. The remains of the fortress are still known by the name of the "Castle of the Jew's Daughter," a name which may well have originated in much later times than that of the Jewish exile here. In any case it is barely worth while to try to prove the identity of this building with Jeremiah's "House of Pharaoh," an expression which the prophet may quite well have used figuratively, and which need not for a moment pre-suppose the real existence of a palace-fort of the king at Daphnae. The excavations showed that the fortress was mainly occupied by Greek mercenary troops, and no Jewish remains of any kind whatsoever were brought to light. This fact does not in any way discredit the narrative of Jeremiah. In the first place, the excavation of the site was not complete. And in the second the sojourn of the Jewish exiles may have been very short. Indeed Josephus preserves a story that Nebuchadnezzar, when he conquered Egypt (in the supposed invasion of 568 B.C.), "took those Jews that were there captive, and led them away to Babylon; and such was the end of the nation of the Hebrews."

CHAPTER IX

THE JEWISH COLONIES IN EGYPT

IF we may trust the evidence of Jeremiah 44.1, there were at the time of the destruction of Jerusalem, or shortly after this event, Jewish colonies in various parts of Egypt, in Migdol, Daphnae, Noph or Memphis, and in the country of Pathros (Southern Egypt). These colonies need not necessarily all have consisted of persons who had left Judah along with Jeremiah. The XXVIth Dynasty had encouraged the settlement of foreigners in the Nile valley, partly as traders, partly as mercenaries in the Egyptian armies. Among those who flocked in there may well have been many Jews, more especially in the period preceding the fall of Jerusalem, when the factions of Assyrophile and Egyptophile were rife. The temporary ascendancy of one party must often have forced prominent members of the other to retire to the country whose interests they supported. Yet of these colonies in Egypt we know nothing, and it is not until the fifth century, after Egypt had become a Persian province, that, through a happy chance, we are given an insight into the daily life of one of them.

In 1904 the antiquity dealers of Aswan, the ancient Syene, 600 miles up the Nile above Cairo, sold to two English buyers a number of papyri written in the Aramaic language, which in Palestine succeeded Hebrew as the speech of the Jewish people. The contents of these papyri made it clear that during the period of the Persian occupation of Egypt a Jewish colony had existed in the town of Yeb or Elephantine, at the south end of a small island lying in the Nile opposite Aswan (Map 1). In 1906 to 1908 excavations undertaken by the Berlin Museum led to the recovery of more papyri of a similar kind, which enable us to reconstruct with certainty the main features of the life of this curious settlement.

Its nature was purely military. Elephantine was the frontier fortress of the south, just as Daphnae and Marea were the frontier fortresses of the Eastern and Western Delta respectively. It was responsible not only for holding in check the Nubians further up the Nile, but also for the maintenance of order throughout Upper Egypt, the biblical Pathros. The garrison consisted partly of Persian soldiery with a Persian commander-in-chief, partly of mercenaries comprising both Jews and other Semites.

The papyri found extend in date from the 27th year of Darius I, 494 B.C., through the reigns of Xerxes, Artaxerxes I and Darius II, down to the fifth year of Amyrtaeus (400 B.C.), the first of the restored Egyptian kings after the throwing off of the Persian yoke. They comprise official documents issued both by the Persian government and by the Jewish community, private business papers, accounts, lists of names, letters and literary texts. The language and script are Aramaic, a Semitic dialect which had already become widespread in Assyrian times, and which the Persians had adopted as the medium of official communication in the western portion of their vast empire. It is not surprising to find this language used in the documents emanating from the Persian government of Egypt, but it is remarkable that it should have been also used in the private documents, for it shows that the Jews who had entered Egypt speaking Hebrew even as late as Jeremiah's time had now adopted Aramaic. Well might Nehemiah (13.23 ff.) complain that in his time children of mixed marriages in Palestine could no longer speak Hebrew.

The Jews of Elephantine had, according to their own account, been settled there since " the days of the kings of Egypt," from which we might infer that they had entered Egypt as mercenaries during the warlike days of the XXVIth Dynasty. The Jews whom Jeremiah mentions (44.1) as scattered over Egypt as far as Pathros (Upper Egypt) were doubtless among these. The Letter of Aristeas, a document with regard to whose value as evidence authorities are divided, states that Psammetichus II, 593-588, used Jewish troops in a campaign against the Ethiopians. The importation of Jewish mercenaries is perhaps to be traced back even further than this. In the book of Deuteronomy, which consists of a body of law promulgated under Josiah in 621 B.C., we read (17.16) among the qualifications required of the King of the Jews " But he shall not multiply horses to himself, nor cause the people to return to Egypt, to the end that he should multiply horses." This passage has puzzled the commentators, but it becomes clear if we follow Meyer in supposing that the kings of Judah had been in the habit of bartering mercenaries for Egyptian horses (see above p. 156).

If this suggestion is correct, the origin of the Jewish diaspora in Egypt would reach back into

the seventh century B.C. This is perhaps con-
firmed by the fact of the existence at Elephantine
of a temple of Yahu (Yahweh), for one of the main
effects of Josiah's legislation was to concentrate
the worship of the Jewish god at Jerusalem, and
to forbid the making of a temple to him in any
other place.

The colony thus formed a religious community
which had its own organization quite apart from
that imposed on it by the Persians in its capacity
of a mercenary garrison. At its head stood a
chief, who in the time of Darius II was one
Yedoniah son of Gemariah. Among the colleagues who assisted the chief in his functions
were " the priests (of Yahu) in the fortress of
Elephantine." The community was divided into
groups each nominally consisting of one hundred
souls ; the whole colony must have numbered
about 600 persons including women and children.

The personal names are mostly those known
to us from the later portions of the Old
Testament ; among them occur from time to
time others, Babylonian, Aramaic or Egyptian.
no fewer than one quarter of the pure Jewish
names are compounded with Yahu. Yet it is
not to be argued from this that Yahu was the
only deity worshipped at Elephantine. We have

already seen reason to believe that the worship
which prevailed had been established by Jews who
left Palestine before the legislation of Josiah
reduced the Jewish religion to what was practically a monotheism.   Thus a papyrus containing
the names of some 120 members of the community
who contributed two shekels each to the common
cult apportions the total sum collected as follows :

> Silver, 31 *karsh* and 8 *seqel.*
> Thereof for Yahu 12 *karsh* and 6 (*sic*) *seqel.*
> for Ashim-betel 7 *karsh.*
> for Anath-betel 12 *karsh.*

The deity Ashim (the vocalization is uncertain)
is probably to be connected with the goddess
Ashima of Samaria, whose worship Amos (writing
about 750 B.C.) reproves in his countrymen,
" They that swear by Ashima[1] of Samaria and say
' By the life of thy god, O Dan,' and ' By the
life of thy deity, O Beersheba ' " (Amos 8.14).

Anath is well known to us from Egyptian
texts as a warrior-goddess of Palestine.   She
gave her name to Bethany " House of Anath,"
and seems to have been especially regarded in

---

1.   The translation of the A.V., " They that swear by the sin of Samaria,"
is manifestly nonsense.   If the rendering given above, due to Gressmann,
is correct, then the statement of II Kings 17.30 that the " men of Hamath
made Ashim " when they were brought in to colonize Samaria after its
depopulation by Sargon of Assyria, in 722 B.C., cannot be literally true.

the neighbourhood of Jerusalem. It has even been suggested that she is identical with the "queen of heaven" against whose worship by the Jewish women both in Upper Egypt and previously in Jerusalem, Jeremiah 44 inveighs so heavily.

Thus we find that Yahu had been accompanied into Egypt by two of the deities who had been worshipped side by side with him in Palestine, though these are regarded as occupying a very inferior position. This is indicated in each case by the addition of the word betel or bethel to the name. Bethel, literally "House of God," is the name of the sacred stone in which the deity is regarded as dwelling. In this case the bethel must be that of Yahu, and the two names "Ashim of the Bethel" and "Anath of the Bethel" clearly show the dependence on him of the two goddesses. This is corroborated by an oath formula where the oath is taken by the goddess "Anath of Yahu."

The most valuable document for the history of this colony of Jews in Egypt is the letter of complaint written by the community in 407 B.C. in reference to the destruction of the temple of Yahu in 410 B.C. This letter is of such import-ance that it may be quoted practically in full.

" To our Lord Bagoas, Governor of Judah. Thy servants Yedoniah and his colleagues, the priests in the fortress of Yeb (Elephantine)." Then follow the usual formulae of greeting. " Thy servants Yedoniah and his colleagues speak as follows :

In the month of Tammuz in year 14 of King Darius (410 B.C.) when Arsames (the Persian governor of Egypt) had left and gone to the King, the priests of the god Khnum in the fortress of Elephantine conspired with Widarnag, who was commander here, to make away with the temple of the god Yahu in the fortress of Yeb. Thereupon this Widarnag, the accursed one, sent a message to his son Nephayan, who was the officer commanding in the fortress of Syene (Aswan), to this effect, ' The temple of the god Yahu in the fortress of Elephantine shall be destroyed.' Thereupon Nephayan brought up Egyptians and other soldiery ; they came to the fortress of Elephantine with their weapons, entered the aforesaid temple and destroyed it even down to the ground, and they broke up the stone columns which were there. They also destroyed the five stone doorways, built of blocks of stone, which were in the aforesaid temple, and their doors and the brazen hinges of those doors ; likewise the roof of cedar wood together with the rest of the fittings and whatsoever else there was they burned with fire. And the gold and silver bowls and all else that was in the temple they removed and appropriated. Our fathers had built the aforesaid temple in the fortress of Yeb in the days of the kings of Egypt, and when Cambyses marched against Egypt he found this temple already built. And though the temples of the gods of Egypt were all destroyed, yet no man did any harm to the aforesaid temple.

And since the time when they did this we and our wives and our children have worn mourning, and fasted and prayed to Yahu, Lord of Heaven. . . .

Once previously, at the time when this evil deed was done to us, we sent a letter to our lord, as also to Jochanan the High Priest, and his colleagues, the priests in Jerusalem, and to Ostanes the brother of Anani, and the principal Jews ; but they have sent us no reply.

Since the month of Tammuz of Year 14 of King Darius until this day we have worn mourning and fasted ; our womenfolk are become as a widow ; we anoint ourselves no more with oil and we drink no wine. Moreover, from that time until now, Year 17 of King Darius, no food-offerings, incense and burnt offerings have been offered in the aforesaid temple.

And now thy servants Yedoniah and his colleagues and the community of Jews, inhabitants of Yeb, say as follows:

If it seem good to our lord may he bethink him of this temple to build it up, for they do not suffer us to build it up. Look upon the receivers of thy benefits and favours here in Egypt. May a despatch be sent for them by thee concerning the temple of the god Yahu, to build it up in the fortress of Yeb even as it was built aforetime, and they will offer the food-offerings and the incense and the burnt offerings upon the altar of the god Yahu in thy name ; and we will at all time pray for thee, we and our wives and children and all the Jews who are here, if so be that this temple shall be built up. And thou shalt win for thyself merit in the sight of Yahu the God of Heaven, more than a man who offers to him burnt-offerings and slaughterings to the value of 1,000 silver talents. And concerning gold we have sent a messenger and given instructions.

We have, moreover, reported the whole matter in a letter in our name to Delaniah and Shelemiah the sons of Sin-uballit, governor of Samaria. Further, Arsames has no knowledge of what has been done to us."

The letter needs little comment for it explains itself. The last paragraph exculpates Arsames, the Persian satrap of Egypt, from all share in the attack on Yahu's temple, and the last words of the previous paragraph clearly hint at a bribe to Bagoas. But who are the addressees ? Bagoas the governor of Jerusalem was already known to us before the discovery of the Elephantine papyri. Josephus records only one piece of Jewish history between the time of Nehemiah and that of Alexander the Great, namely that the High Priest Jochanan, grandson of Eliashib, who held the office in the days of Nehemiah, slew his own brother Jesus in the temple at Jerusalem, fearing that the latter, being a friend of Bagoas " the general of Artaxerxes," might be set in his place. This Bagoas had previously been identified with the great Persian minister who controlled the policy of Persia in the later years of Artaxerxes III (359-338 B.C.). But our papyrus makes it clear that this is incorrect, and that the Bagoas of Josephus is identical with him to whom the letter of the Jews of Yeb was written, for the letter actually mentions Jochanan as High Priest.

Bagoas then must have been a successor of Nehemiah as governor of Jerusalem who was in office in 407 B.C. and who, therefore, is hardly to be identified with the great minister of Artaxerxes III's reign fifty years later.

Of Ostanes, brother of Anani, we know nothing. His Persian name need not indicate Persian nationality, the more so as his brother's name is Jewish.

The addressees whose appearance most surprises us are Delaniah and Shelemiah, sons of Sin-uballit, governor of Samaria. Their father is clearly Nehemiah's opponent Sanballat, who did so much to prevent the rebuilding of the temple of Jerusalem (Neh. 4.1, etc.). Nehemiah never gives him the title of governor of Samaria, though it is clear from 4.2 that he held a position of some importance there. In 407 B.C. Sanballat must, if still living, have been of considerable age, and it may be for this reason that his sons are appealed to.

But why should the Jews of Elephantine appeal to Samaritans at all ? Not a generation previously the Samaritans had been foremost in opposing the rebuilding of the Temple at Jerusalem, and though they had accepted the legislation of Nehemiah in 433 B.C. the breach

had never been entirely healed. It would thus
seem hardly likely that their influence would go
far to secure the Egyptian Jews a favourable
hearing at Jerusalem. Some would meet this
difficulty by supposing that the Elephantine
Jews were of Samaritan origin. Of this there is
no proof. Another possibility is suggested by
Neh. 13.28, where we read that one of the
grandsons of Eliashib the High Priest was son-in-
law to Sanballat. Thus Sanballat's family was
connected by marriage with the High Priestly
family in Jerusalem, and so it may be that his
sons had influence in that quarter. If this is so
a reconciliation between the two families must
have taken place since Nehemiah's time, for the
verse referred to above concerning Eliashib's
grandson ends "therefore I chased him from
me." In any case it should be remembered that
what was needed for the rebuilding of the
Elephantine temple was not merely the permission of the High Priest of Jerusalem, but also
that of the Persian governor Bagoas. It may
have been with this latter that the Samaritans
were believed to have influence.

The preamble of the first reply of Bagoas and
Delaniah has fortunately been preserved. The
instructions of the bearer are " to speak in Egypt

concerning the altar-house of the God of Heaven which was formerly built in the fortress of Yeb, . . . to build it up in its place as it was aforetime, and they shall bring food-offerings and incense on that altar even as it happened formerly."

It is clear from this that the Jewish arguments, whether logical or metallic, had prevailed in Palestine. It is equally clear that the omission of all reference to burnt offerings as opposed to unburnt food-offerings is intentional. The Jews had specifically requested permission to offer three kinds of offering; permission is granted in the case of food-offerings and incense, and withheld in the case of burnt offerings. That the omission was important is shown by a fragment of another appeal, possibly of later date, by five of the Jews to some influential person not actually named. In it we find the following words, " If our lord (the addressee) [intercedes for us?] and if the temple of Yahu [is rebuilt] as it was before, and if sheep, oxen and goats . . . are not offered there, but only incense and food-offerings . . . we will deliver to the house of our lord 1000 bushels of corn." It is not easy to see why the permission for burnt offerings was refused. The position of Bagoas was doubtless far from easy, so much so that he had spent three years without taking action at all. On the one side was his Persian master, on the other the Jews of Palestine, who doubtless resented the existence of a temple of Yahweh outside Jerusalem. It may have been in an attempt to propitiate these last that the name of Yahweh was so significantly omitted from his reply quoted above. Yet again he had to pacify the Egyptians, who were probably not too well disposed towards the foreign worship of the Jews in their midst, as their destruction of the temple had abundantly shown. Was it in deference to these that the permission to make burnt offerings was withheld ? It is hardly likely. Our evidence, though scanty, is conclusive as to the fact that the Egyptians themselves made burnt offerings, and, though the animals sacrificed by the Jews, the ox, the sheep and the goat, were all regarded as sacred in some part of Egypt or other, none of these was worshipped locally at Elephantine with the exception of the sheep, the local god Khnum being represented with the head of a ram, a fact which may indeed have helped towards the destruction of Yahweh's temple in 410 B.C. It is perhaps more likely that burnt animal sacrifice was regarded as an offence against the Persian religion of fire-worship, for the teaching of Zoroaster was that the sacred element of fire was polluted by contact with the animal bodies.

Whether the community of Yeb ever re-built their sanctuary we never learn, for only two years later, 405 B.C., occurred the revolt of Egypt against her Persian conquerors and her liberation from the yoke. That our community survived this is clear from a document dated in Year 5 of Amyrtaeus the first king of the restored Egypt. But with this the history of the colony appears to end.

It hardly falls within the compass of a work of this nature to describe at length the internal conditions prevailing in the colony of Yeb as illustrated by the private documents, or to deal with the marriage contracts of Mibhtahyah the daughter of Mahseiah, or with her dowry and her trousseau on the occasions of her two marriages. It is impossible, however, to pass unnoticed another official document, the permission granted by Darius in 419 B.C. for the holding of the Feast of Unleavened Bread.

This document is in the form of a letter from a certain Jew, Khananiah, to the Jewish community in Yeb. It contains an account of an official instruction sent by Darius II to the Persian

governor of Egypt, Arsames, and perhaps brought
to Egypt by Khananiah himself. Unfortunately
half of most of the lines has been lost, and the
filling in of the lacunae thus formed must be a
matter of considerable uncertainty. The letter
is addressed " To my brother Yedoniah and his
colleagues, the Jewish army, your brother
Khananiah." It reads as follows :

" [To my brother] Yedoniah and his colleagues,
the Jewish army, your brother Khananiah. May
God bless you. In this year, Year 5 of King
Darius, instructions have been sent from the
King to Arsames. . . . 'You are now to count
thus ; fourteen [days of Nisan] . . . and from
day 15 to day 21 of [Nisan]. . . . Be ye pure
(?) and beware. Ye shall do no work. . . . Ye
shall not drink [beer], nor [shall ye] . . . anything
in which is leaven . . . from the going down of
the sun [on the 15th of Nisan] until the 21st of
Nisan . . . [ye shall not] bring it into your rooms.
And ye shall make a separation between the
days. . . ."

In the eyes of many scholars the significance
of this document lies in the absence of all reference
to the Passover proper, with its sacrifice of a
lamb and the meal which followed this. The
Jewish Feast of the Passover clearly comprehended

two festivals entirely separate in origin, firstly, a very primitive ceremony in which a lamb was slain and its blood smeared on the door-posts of each house, and secondly, a feast which took place at the time of the beginning of the barley harvest, and the chief ceremony in which was the eating of unleavened bread. Both these feasts took place in the spring, and by a process which need not here be described, they became united into a single feast in which a lamb was killed towards sundown on the 14th day of Abib (pre-exilic calendar), and eaten the same evening, *i.e.* the evening of the 15th according to Jewish reckoning; on this followed at once the seven days of unleavened bread, from the 14th to the 21st, the first[1] and last of which were holy and no work was done on them.

In the decalogue of Exodus 34 and the Book of the Covenant of Exodus 23 the two feasts are still clearly distinct. But in Deuteronomy 16 they are already combined, and the Passover-lamb is only to be slaughtered at the Temple in Jerusalem, not in the private houses. This last must have been an unendurable hardship, and we find that the Priestly Codex as exemplified

---

[1] Note, however, that Deuteronomy 16.8 mentions no holy day on the first day but only on the seventh.

by Exodus 12 returns to the old custom of a family Passover-lamb.

Some authorities see in the absence from Darius' proclamation of any reference to the sacrifice of the lamb a proof of the fact that at this time the sacrifice was made only in the Temple at Jerusalem. It must be confessed that this reasoning is not altogether convincing. In the first place the argument is a negative one, and though there is a probability that a document prescribing in detail how the combined Passover-Unleavened-Bread-Feast should be observed would have dealt with the question of the sacrifice had such existed, it is not quite a certainty. In the second place Naville may be right in attacking Eduard Meyer's assumption that these ordinances were intended not for Elephantine alone but for the Jews of the whole Persian Empire. There was indeed a special reason why the sacrifice of a lamb, harmless enough at Migdol or Daphnae, might be very obnoxious at Elephantine, for the local Egyptian god was Khnum, who is represented under the form of a ram.

We do not know the eventual fate of the Jewish military colony at Yeb. Some have supposed that it perished, or came nigh to perishing, in the revolt of Egypt against Persia in 405 B.C. A sadly damaged papyrus contains a list of names headed by Yedoniah, son of Gemariah, " who were found at the door and killed (??) " and a list of women possibly carried off prisoners. But the document is undated, and its translation and bearing are quite uncertain. We can only be sure that the colony was still in existence in 400 B.C., from which date we have a statement of debt made by a Jew, Menakhem, son of Shallum, an Aramaean of the fortress of Yeb, against a Jewess, Selua.

CHAPTER X

THE EPISODE OF ONIAS

On the death of Alexander the Great in 323 B.C.
the vast empire which he had conquered in the
East was divided up among his generals. Egypt
fell to Ptolemy, who founded there the line known
as that of the Lagides, which ruled Egypt until
the country became a Roman province in 29 B.C.
Syria was taken over by Antigonus, who, however,
was dispossessed by Seleucus in 301 B.C., after the
battle of Ipsus. Seleucus became by this victory
master not only of Syria but also of parts of
Asia Minor, of Babylonia and of Assyria, and the
line which he founded, the Seleucids, ruled this
wide empire for nearly two centuries.

Under the earlier kings of this house the Jews
had experienced very considerable religious
toleration. It has been said that they went
into captivity a political society and returned a
church, and it is at least true that during the
period which followed the return from Babylon
they approximated most closely to the ideal of a
kingdom of priests. In 175 B.C. Antiochus

Epiphanes ascended the throne of Syria, and very unwisely departed from the example of his predecessors by trying to force on the Jews conformity with the Hellenistic practices both civil and religious. At this moment Onias III was High Priest in Judea, and his brother Jason or Jesus was the leader of a powerful Hellenizing faction in the country, whose policy was to betray the old theocratic party to Antiochus for its own profit. Jason began by offering the king a bribe to establish him in the High Priesthood. Antiochus, anxious to weld his empire into one homogeneous whole by introducing Greek ideas throughout, readily accepted the offer, and Jason, by neglecting the Temple worship and generally encouraging Greek ideas, appears to have performed his share of the compact. In 172 B.C., however, Jason was outbidden for the High Priesthood by his own ambassador to the king, Menelaus. Not to be outdone, he attacked Jerusalem in 168 B.C. with a force of 1000 men. It was at this moment that Antiochus returned in no pleasant humour from Egypt, where the Roman legate Popilius had forbidden him to carry out his projected attack on Ptolemy, the Egyptian king, unless he wished to face another meeting with the dreaded

Roman legions. Determined to put an end to these civil broils, he took Jerusalem by storm and massacred many of the inhabitants. An altar of Olympian Zeus was set up in the city, the Temple of Jehovah was re-dedicated to that god, and the Jews were forced to observe the festival of Dionysus. Every student of Jewish history knows the sequel, the rise of the Maccabees and their courageous fight against the Syrian kings, as a result of which the Jews attained not only religious but also civil liberty.

For the moment, however, we are to leave the main stream of Jewish story and follow one of its backwaters, which once again leads us into Egypt. Onias III, whom Jason had deposed, and who had finally been murdered in 172 B.C., had a son known to historians as Onias IV. About 162 B.C. the new king of Syria, Antiochus Eupator, appointed as High Priest in Jerusalem one Alkimos, who did not belong to the priestly family. The young Onias, disgusted with the turn which events had taken, and apprehensive that the new priestly family might make their own succession the more secure by murdering him, fled to Egypt, to the court of Ptolemy Philometor and Cleopatra his queen. The rest of his story is told by Josephus. We need not regard as genuine the letter which Onias wrote to Ptolemy requesting permission to build a temple " to Almighty God " at Leontopolis, nor yet Ptolemy's answer, in which Onias is given permission " to purge an old temple which had fallen into ruins at Leontopolis, in the nome of Heliopolis, and which is named after Bubastis Agria." The letters are doubtless historical forgeries of Josephus after the manner of Thucydides' speeches, but about the facts there is no doubt. " So Onias took the place, and built a temple, and an altar to God, like indeed to that at Jerusalem, but smaller and poorer." In his *Wars of the Jews* Josephus gives us further details about this temple. The place lay 180 *stadia* from Memphis, in the nome of Heliopolis, " where Onias built a fortress and a temple, not like to that at Jerusalem, but such as resembled a tower. He built it of large stones to the height of 60 cubits ; he made the structure of the altar in imitation of that in our own country, and in like manner adorned with gifts, . . . but the entire temple was encompassed with a wall of burnt brick, though it had gates of stone." Josephus further tells us that this temple was finally closed by Paulinus the Roman governor of Alexandria shortly after the capture of

Jerusalem by Titus in 70 A.D. His statement that it was open for 343 years in all is an obvious error of calculation.

Egyptian history unfortunately throws no light on this incident. Excavation claims to have been more successful. About twenty miles north of Cairo lies a site called Tell el-Yahudiyeh, the Mound of the Jewess (Map 2). It was first excavated in 1887 by Naville and Griffith, who found there antiquities of various Egyptian periods, and a cemetery with gravestones some of which bore Jewish proper names. In 1906 further excavations were carried out in the mound by Petrie. A vast walled encampment of the Hyksos period was discovered, together with the cemetery of its inhabitants. In addition to this a building was found, constructed on an artificial mound, which Petrie identifies with the Temple of Onias.

Is this identification correct ? There are two questions to be considered, not entirely independent the one of the other. Firstly, is Tell el-Yahudiyeh the site described by Josephus, and secondly, is the building found by Petrie the temple of Onias.

Josephus tells us that Onias built his temple at Leontopolis, in the Heliopolite nome, in a fortified place "named after Bubastis Agria," while in another passage the ruined temple referred to in the letter to Ptolemy and Cleopatra is said to be "named after Bubastis Agria." Now Leontopolis is the "City of the Lion" and the most natural translation of the words "Bubastis Agria" is "the Fierce Bast,"[1] namely that form of the cat-headed goddess Bast which was identified with the lion-headed goddess Sekhmet. Tell el-Yahudiyeh, to judge by its position, may well have been in the Heliopolite nome, and if we can show that Sekhmet the lion-headed goddess was worshipped there we shall have made out a strong presumptive case for the identification. The sole piece of evidence which points in this direction is a statue found on the site by Petrie. It is the figure of an admiral called Hor who served under Psammetichus II, and who is represented as holding up a shrine in which is a cat- or lion-headed goddess, clearly some form of Bast. This figure was found in the city, but not in a temple, indeed

---

[1] The translation "Bubastis of the Fields" is barely possible, and Naville's further proposal to identify this with a goddess Sekhet-neter (in which Sekhet is written with the field-sign), followed by Petrie, is not to be accepted, for this goddess has no real existence. In the inscription Naville, *Bubastis*, Pl. XLIII.A the words simply mean " The Divine Field," and Naville has turned them into a god by combining with them the next sign (the snake-sign) as determinative of deity, whereas in reality this goes with what follows, " priestess of the goddess Uto."

the excavator uses it to prove the existence of
a temple of Bast here in the XXVIth Dynasty.
The presence of a figure of Bast in a town does
not prove conclusively that that town was devoted
to the worship of Bast, for it may have been
brought there from elsewhere ; still less does it
prove that the town was in Greek times called
Leontopolis " City of the Lion-headed Goddess,"
for not every town in which Bast was worshipped
was called Leontopolis. At the same time the
presence of the figure is a piece of evidence
which must not be under-rated.

Josephus states that the place given to Onias
lay 180 *stadia* from Memphis. The Greek
stadion, which one would naturally expect
Josephus to employ, is rather more than 600
English feet in length, and 180 of these would
not nearly take us from Memphis to Tell el-
Yahudiyeh. In order to avoid this difficulty
Petrie supposes Josephus to have intended by
the *stadion* an Egyptian measure of 500 cubits,
various multiples of which are marked off by stone
pillars along the desert road from Saqqara to
the Fayyum. Of such *stadia* he states that there
would be 186 from Tell el-Yahudiyeh to the
north gate of Memphis. To suppose that
Josephus, writing in Greek for readers whose

language was Greek, used an Egyptian measure and called it by the name *stadion*, without warning his readers that he did not refer to the ordinary Greek *stadion*, is a very large assumption, and the fact is that this figure of 180 *stadia* is a serious difficulty in the identification of Leontopolis with Tell el-Yahudiyeh, at any rate for those who are inclined to take Josephus' figures very seriously.

The fact that the mound is called Tell el-Yahudiyeh is worth nothing as evidence. Names of this type are not rare in the Eastern Delta. At Daphnae (Tell Defenneh) we have a mound called Qasr Bint el-Yahudi " The Castle of the Daughter of the Jew," and not sixteen miles north-east of Tell el-Yahudiyeh itself is another mound called Tell Yahud " The Mound of Jews." There were no doubt Jewish colonies in many other towns of the Eastern Delta besides Daphnae, and for this same reason we cannot take the presence of Jewish burials at Tell el-Yahudiyeh as proof that this site was that of Onias.

Thus the evidence for the identification of Tell el-Yahudiyeh with the site allotted to Onias must be admitted to be far from conclusive. At the same time could Petrie show us the Temple of Onias itself on the site there would be no further reason for doubt. Has he done this?

The site had been occupied in Hyksos times by a large rectangular fortified enclosure, a mile in circumference. The rampart consisted mainly of sand, with a sloping face on the outer side covered with a coating of hard white plaster. Outside this had been added, at a later date, a stone wall of fine white limestone, which has been completely destroyed, partly in ancient, partly in modern times.

Outside the north-east corner of this camp lies an artificial mound about 70 feet in maximum height and roughly triangular in form. The north side of the triangle runs almost due east and west and is 716 feet in length. The east side, running due north and south, is 788 feet in length. The third side is irregular and slightly concave, its general direction being north-west and south-east. In order to hold together the material of which the mound was composed it was revetted on all sides. On the north the revetment was of mud brick, which had been burnt red in some subsequent conflagration; on the east it consists of a fine wall of stone; on the west it has almost entirely disappeared, but the slight traces which remain show it to have been of brick.

On the northern or lower portion of the summit of this mound once lay a small town, the houses of which have been completely destroyed. There were two modes of access to the town, one by a stone gateway in the north-west corner, and the other by a long stairway 14 feet wide in the centre of the east side.

At the highest point of the mound, just south of the head of this stairway, lies a group of buildings which Petrie identifies with the Temple of Onias. An enclosure wall, rather boldly restored by the excavator from very minute remains, appears to bound the temple area on the east side. The temple itself consists of a long narrow structure running roughly N.N.W.-S.S.E., entered from the north end, and containing three rooms, an outer court, an inner court and a sanctuary or temple proper.

This structure has been almost completely destroyed. Nothing remains of the outer and inner courts except portions of the foundations of their outer walls, which were probably of brickwork plastered over. The wall which divided the two courts may have been of stone, for nothing now remains save the trench into which it was set. Of the temple proper there has survived only its foundation platform of mud brick, solid except for a space of a foot up the main axis. The platform measures 658 inches by 201.

North of the temple buildings and at the head of the great eastern stairway are indications in the ground which led the excavator to restore a rectangular building about 73 by 52 feet. This he calls the Citadel. It stands on the highest point of the mound and commands the stairway, the temple courts, and the town on the north half of the mound.

Such is, in brief, the description of what Petrie found, and he is of opinion that the site is nothing other than the Mound of Onias with its temple. He points out that the place and the buildings fit in very reasonably with Josephus' description. Thus the fortress mentioned as already existing here would be the Hyksos camp, the stone from the later wall of which might well have been used by Onias for his work. The burnt wall to the north would account for Josephus' story that the temple was surrounded by a wall of burnt brick, and the fortifications with the commanding tower would justify his calling it a fort (*phrourion*). His description of it as like a tower (*purgon*) well might be due to the impression made by the lofty retaining walls of the mound, surmounted by those of the temple buildings and the keep, and Petrie has by a not unreasonable calculation worked out the height of the temple roof as very close on 60 cubits from the ground level. He points out, moreover, that the platform of the sanctuary, 658 inches long by 201 broad, approximates in shape fairly closely to the Temple of Solomon, which measured 70 cubits by 20.[1] If, moreover, we allow a footing of half a cubit (between 9 and 10 inches) between the edge of the platform and outer edge of the walls which were based on it we should get a room whose outer measurements were 638 by 182 inches, which is almost precisely 35 cubits by 10, or half the linear measurements of Solomon's Temple. May it not well be that Onias, unable to build on the lordly scale of Solomon, simply halved the measurements, or, in other words, is not the fact of these dimensions being so exactly half of those at Jerusalem a good reason for identifying the building with the temple of Onias, " like, indeed, to that at Jerusalem, but smaller and poorer." Petrie goes even further than this and sees in the general shape and arrangement of the mound an attempt to reproduce the topographical

---

[1] Only, however, if we include the porch (I Kings 6.2-3).

features of Jerusalem. The parallel is far from convincing and we may agree with Petrie himself when he says that it " might seem fanciful, were we not certain of the nature of the place."

But are we so certain ? It is true that we have found that certain of Josephus' descriptions might conceivably be made to apply to Tell el-Yahudiyeh, but it is not without making very liberal allowances. Thus Josephus actually says that the entire temple was encompassed with a wall of burnt brick, which was manifestly not the case. He states that the temple (not the fortress) was built of large stones to the height of 60 cubits, though all that remains in position of the temple, including the walls of the outer and inner court, is actually of brick, and even if the various stone columns and capitals of which fragments were found by Petrie below the mound actually belonged to this temple it could never have been accurately described as " built of large stones." In fact we cannot avoid the conclusion that Josephus' description of the temple of Onias, if this be it, is very far from accurate. It is not even consistent, for in the *Antiquities* he describes the building as " like, indeed, to that at Jerusalem, but smaller and poorer," while in the *Wars* it is " not like to that

at Jerusalem, but such as resembled a tower."
It is, therefore, very doubtful whether any
attempt to identify this building on Josephus'
general description of it can ever be successful,
and we must, therefore, fall back on other
arguments.

It is, indeed, striking that the dimensions of
the brick platform which forms the foundation
of the sanctuary should be so nearly half of those
of Solomon's temple. But for purposes of
argument all the value is taken out of the resemblance when we remember that the temple at
Jerusalem which Onias copied, if he copied any,
was not that of Solomon, which had been
destroyed some centuries previously, but that
begun by Zerubbabel, which we have no reason
for supposing to have had the same dimensions
as that of Solomon. Indeed, there is evidence
to the contrary, for Josephus tells us that Herod,
in his speech to the people on the foundation of
his temple, exonerated Zerubbabel and his
fellow builders from all blame for having built
their temple 60 cubits lower than that of Solomon,
stating that they had obeyed the measures given
them by Cyrus and Darius. It is true that only
the height is here mentioned as having been
different, but in Ezra 6.3 we read that the

breadth was 60 cubits, as against the 20 of Solomon's. This evidence may not be of the highest value, but, such as it is, it justifies no attempt to assume that Zerubbabel's temple, which Onias copied, was of the same size as Solomon's. The argument from the proportions and absolute dimensions of the platform at Tell el-Yahudiyeh therefore falls to the ground.

It may still be argued that even though definite proof of the identity of the building on Tell el-Yahudiyeh with Onias' temple cannot be found, yet it is highly probable. Even this is doubtful. Let it be granted that this mound was piled some time during the second century B.C., that the heaping up of such mounds was not a procedure used by Egyptian architects, that some of the details are un-Egyptian, notably the drafting of the stones in the eastern retaining wall, and the cornices and battlements; grant that there are Jews buried in the cemetery found here by Naville, and that on a potsherd inscribed in Egyptian demotic and bearing certain accounts relating to the furnishing of bricks we find the names Abram and Shabtai. If all this be granted it amounts to nothing more than that, at some time in the second century B.C., a colony of foreigners lived there, consisting in part of Jews, and built a fortress and a building which may possibly have been a temple. There were many colonies of foreigners in Egypt in the second century, many Jews among them, and many fortresses and garrisons in the Delta. It may be significant, though negative evidence is never entirely to be trusted, that among the remains of the houses on the mound the earliest coins found were not of Onias' time[1], about 154 B.C., but of the reign of Ptolemy Soter II, who came to the throne in 117 B.C., more than a generation later.

But, it may be asked, is not the whole matter clinched by the passover-ovens found by Petrie in the base of the mound? To this it is to be replied that the term passover-oven is a question-begging compound. The objects to which Petrie gave this name were found in various places at the base of the mound, enveloped in the earth of which it is composed. They are cylindrical jars of pottery roughly two feet wide and two and a half high, rather narrower at the open top than at the bottom. Sometimes they were bricked round and coated with mud plaster, and in some cases they had, before use, apparently been let into the ground. At the bottom of each

[1] The statement in Knight, *Nile and Jordan*, p. 157, to the effect that " coins of Onias " were found here is incorrect.

jar was from one to three inches of wood ash ;
" bones of lambs lay upon the ashes, usually burnt,
sometimes unburnt." The jars had no lids, but
were of course full of the earth of which the mound
was composed.

For Petrie these jars represent the remains of
a Passover feast, but one of a special nature,
celebrated to mark the foundation of the New
Jerusalem in Egypt. He believes that after the
roasting of the lambs earth was thrown over the
the ovens so as to smother the fires ; " thus they
began to found the new city in the dying flames
of sacrifice." " There was a deep meaning in
this," he adds, " though not strictly orthodox.
The Canaanites had sacrificed a child to place
beneath their buildings : in the Jewish age it is
found in Palestine that a lighted lamp was covered[1]
with a bowl, and then built over with the foundations, thus killing a flame of fire instead of a life.
Here this fire-killing was done on the largest
scale, and the whole mound rests upon the
extinguished fires of the sacrifices."

Now when Petrie states that such a procedure
is " not strictly orthodox " he is correct. We
might go further and say that it is most unorth-
odox. Whatever may have been the original

[1] By Canaanites, be it noted, not by Jews.

P

meaning of the Passover we know that from
at least the ninth century B.C. onward it was
believed to celebrate the deliverance from Egypt.
We should, therefore, hardly expect to find it
used as a foundation ceremony. Onias, too,
might well have been reproached with a lack of
the sense of the fitting if he had proposed to
celebrate by a feast which commemorated the
deliverance from Egypt the foundation of a
building which marked the abandonment by
himself and his followers of the promised land
and their return to the land of bondage. What
is more, we have no evidence for the use, by the
Jews, of a foundation sacrifice of any kind, be it
of a human being or of a living flame, though,
once again, negative evidence is not final. But
in any case it would be a long and illogical step
from the burial, in the foundations, of lighted
lamps at certain fixed points, to the burying of
large numbers of ovens.

We shall, therefore, be wise to rid our minds
of the idea that these jars are " passover-ovens."
That they are ovens is beyond doubt. They
may even mark some special feast held at the
time when the piling of the mound was begun,
but such feast could hardly be a Passover. In
all probability the explanation is something much

simpler, and, despite the fact that they seem to occur only in the base of the mound, it is perhaps unwise to discard entirely the possibility that they were merely the ovens of the community who built it.

Petrie has, indeed, made out a clever case for the identity of Tell el-Yahudiyeh with the Mound of Onias the Jew, but it is a case which when closely examined fails to carry complete conviction, and it may well be that the ruins of Onias' temple still await the spade of some fortunate explorer.

BIBLIOGRAPHY

The following is a brief list of books dealing with the subject. It will be understood that they represent but a fraction of those consulted by the writer in the preparation of this volume.

ENGLISH

BURNEY, C. F. *The Book of Judges.* London, 1918.

———. *Israel's Settlement in Canaan* (Schweich Lectures for 1917). London, 1918.

DRIVER, S. R. *The Book of Genesis,* 11th edit. London, 1920.

———. *The Book of Exodus* (The Cambridge Bible). Cambridge, 1918.

GARDINER, A. H. *The Delta Residence of the Ramessides,* in *Journal of Egyptian Archaeology,* Vol. V. London, 1918.

———. *The Ancient Military Road between Egypt and Palestine ; ibidem,* Vol. VI, pp. 99 ff. London, 1920.

HALL, H. R. *The Ancient History of the Near East,* 4th edit. London, 1919.

KNIGHT, G. A. F. *Nile and Jordan.* London, 1921.

HOMMEL, FRITZ. *The Ancient Hebrew Tradition as illustrated by the Monuments,* translated by E. McClure and L. Crosslé. 1897.

McNEILE, A. H. *The Book of Exodus.* London, 1908.

NAVILLE, E. *Archaeology of the Old Testament.* London, 1913.

————. *The Store-city of Pithom and the Route of the Exodus* (Egypt Exploration Fund). London, 1903.

————. *The Mound of the Jew and the City of Onias* (Egypt Exploration Fund). London, 1890.

————. *The Shrine of Saft el Henneh and the Land of Goshen* (Egypt Exploration Fund). London, 1888.

PETRIE, W. M. F. *Egypt and Israel.* London, 1912.

————. *Hyksos and Israelite Cities.* London, 1906.

SAYCE, A. H. *Patriarchal Palestine.* London, 1895.

————. *The 'Higher Criticism' and the Verdict of the Monuments.* London, 5th edit, 1913.

———— and COWLEY, A. E. *Aramaic Papyri discovered at Assuan.* London, 1906.

FRENCH

DHORME, PAUL. *Les Pays Bibliques et L'Assyrie* (*Revue Biblique*, 1910-11). Paris, 1911.

WEILL, RAYMOND. *La Presqu'île du Sinai.* Paris, 1908.

GERMAN

MEYER, EDUARD. *Die Israeliten und ihre Nachbarstämme.* 1906.

————. *Der Papyrusfund von Elephantine.* Leipzig, 1912.

ALT, A. *Israel und Aegypten.* Leipzig, 1909.

BÖHL, F. *Kanaanäer und Hebräer.* Leipzig, 1911.

SACHAU, EDUARD. *Aramäische Papyrus und Ostraka aus einer Jüdischen Militär-Kolonie zu Elephantine.* Leipzig, 1911.

SPIEGELBERG, W. *Der Aufenthalt Israels in Aegypten.* Strassburg, 1904.

————. *Aegyptische Randglossen zum Alten Testament.*

INDEX

Aahmes, admiral, 94*n*.
Aahmes I, 72, 94*n*.
Aamu (Syrians), 38, 61, 62.
Abdakhiba, 115, 117, 119.
Abijah, 163.
Abram, 20, 27, 39, 47 ff., 223.
abrech, meaning of, 103.
Adad-nirari II, 167.
Adam, 17.
Africanus, 25.
Ahab, 54, 111, 168.
abū, meaning of, 103.
'Ain Gadis, 128.
'Ain Naba, 132-3.
Akaba, Gulf of, 129, 144.
Akhenaton, 146.
Akhetaton, 113, 114.
Akkadia, 56.
Alexander the Great, 209.
Altaqu, 175-6.
Amenemhet I, 38-9, 46, 53.
Amenemhet III, 62.
Amenhotp I, 43.
Amenhotp II, 76, 112, 113.
Amenhotp III, 109, 113, 151.
Amenhotp IV, 146.
Ameny, 38, 53, 62.
Ammi-zaduga, 53.
Ammurabi, 50.
Amon, 71, 146-8, 160.
Amos, 194.
Amraphel, 28, 49-53, 55.
Amyrtaeus, 191, 204.
Anani, 197, 200.
Anastasi V, Papyrus, 142.
Anastasi VI, Papyrus, 65, 76, 82, 88.
Anath, 194.
Antigonus, 209.
Antiochus Epiphanes, 209-210.
Antiochus Eupator, 211.
Aper, 125.
Aperiu, see Aperu.
Aperu, 123-5.
Apophis, 70.
Apries, 185-6.
Arabia, 56, 57, 118, 129, 165, 172.
Aramaeans, 118, 119, 168.

Aramaic language, 191.
Aramaic papyri, 190 ff.
Arioch, 49-50.
Aristeas, Letter of, 192.
Arsames, 196, 199, 205.
Artaxerxes, 199.
Artaxerxes I, 191.
Artaxerxes III, 199, 200.
Asa, 163-6.
Asenath, 97, 100-1.
Ashdod, 173-4, 181.
Asher, tribe of, 110.
Ashim, 194.
Ashima, 194.
Ashkelon, 181.
Ashurbanipal, 172, 178-9, 180.
Ashur-nasir-pal III, 168.
Askalon, 109.
Assyria, 167, 168, 170, 173.
Aswan, 141, 190.
Aton (deity), 113.
Avaris, 68, 69, 70, 72, 73, 85, 90.
Azotus, 181.

Baal-zephon, 135-6, 140, 143.
Baba, 94*n*.
Babylon, 49, 52, 56, 57, 184, 185, 186, 188.
Babylonia, 17, 25, 45, 52, 57, 58, 151, 180.
Bagoas, 196, 199-202.
Bast, 214-5.
Beby, tomb of, 94.
Ben-hadad II, 54, 111, 168.
Beni Hasan, 60, 70.
Betane, 80.
Bethany, 194.
Bethel, 47, 195.
Boghaz Keui, 117.
Brick-making, 99.
Bubastis, 102*n*.
Bubastis Agria, 212-3-4.
Burnt offerings, 202.
Byblos, 148.

Cambyses, 197.
Camels, 60, 165.

Canaan, 21, 26, 27, 49, 55, 56, 57, 76, 102, 109, 110, 118.
Canaanites, 47, 152-3, 225.
Carchemish, 182-3-4.
Carmel, 115.
Carnarvon Tablet, 71
Censorinus, 42.
Chedorlaomer, 49, 51.
Chellus, 80.
Chronology, 23 ff., 41 ff., 54-5, 111-2, 120-1.
Cilicia, 156-7, 168.
Cleopatra, 211.
Coat, Joseph's, 61.
Coptic versions, 34.
Country of the Sea, 52.
Creation, 17.
Cyrus, 222.

DAMASCUS, 54, 111, 168.
Daphnae, 80, 141, 186-190, 216.
Darius I, 191, 193, 196-7-8, 204, 207.
Darius II, 191.
David, 149, 150.
Deborah, Song of, 32.
Delaniah, 198, 200-1.
Dhouthotp, tomb of, 62.
Diodorus, 185.
Diodorus Siculus, 97.
Dionysus, 211.
Duplication in tradition, 47.

E, DOCUMENT, 26, 31, 32, 130, 131, 132, 133.
Ebers Papyrus, 43.
Edom, 65, 129, 130, 149.
Elam, 49-50, 52.
El-'Arish, 138.
El-Bersheh, 62.
Elephantine, 190 ff.
Eliakim, 183.
Eliashib, 199, 201.
Elim, 131-2, 133.
El-Kab, 37, 90.
El-Kantareh, 138.
Ellasar, 49-50-51.
Elohim, 31.
Eriaku, 50-51.
Ero, 87-8.
Esarhaddon, 177.
Etham, 132, 135, 139.

Ethiopians, 80, 157, 159, 165, 169, 173-4-5, 179.
Et-Til, 113.
Euphrates, 57, 112, 182-3.
Eusebius, 25.
Eve, 17.
Ezion-geber, 132.

FAMINES, 48, 95.
Faran, 133.
Fayyum, 215.
Feast of Unleavened Bread, 204-8.
Field of Abram, 162.
Flood, 17.

GAZA, 138, 168, 170, 181.
Gebel Musa, 131, 132.
Gebel Serbal, 131.
Gebel Silsileh, 162.
Gedaliah, 186.
Gemariah, 193, 208.
Genubath, 149.
Gerar, 164, 166.
Gezer, 109, 152-3-4-5, 163.
Goiim, 51.
Goshen, 73, 76, 78 ff., 84, 89, 134.
Greek mercenaries, 188.
Greek states, 180.
Greek version (see Septuagint).

HADAD, 149-151, 158.
Hadad-idri, 54, 111, 168.
Hamath, 168, 183, 194 n.
Hanum, 170.
Hapi, 95.
Haran, 47, 57-8-9.
Harris 500, Papyrus, 123.
Harris Papyrus, the Great, 124.
Hatshepsut, 70.
Hawwarah, 132.
Hebrew version, 26, 27, 33, 82.
Hebrews, 115 ff., 124-5, 188.
Heliopolis, 97-8, 212, 213.
Herakleopolis, 39.
Hero, 87-8.
Herodotus, 87, 97, 176, 182, 185.
Heroonpolis, 79, 87, 135.
Hezekiah, 175.
Hittites, 51, 114, 117, 157.
Hophra, 185.
Hor, 214.
Horeb, 31, 130.

Horemheb, 147.
Horemsaf, 162.
Horses in Egypt, 93, 155-157, 192.
Horus, 101.
Hoshea, 169, 170.
Hrihor, 148.
Human sacrifice, 225.
Hyksos, 67 ff., 93-4, 96-7-8, 213, 217, 223.

Ibsha, 60, 63.
Ipsus, battle of, 209.
Irkhuleni, 168.
Isaac, 20, 55, 118.
Israel, 158, 160-1, 170.

J, Document, 26, 31, 32, 127-8, 130, 131, 132, 133.
Jacob, 20, 28, 47, 54-55, 67, 78, 79, 82, 83, 90, 110.
Jacob-el, 110 n.
Jason, 210.
Jehoahaz, 183.
Jehoiachin, 185.
Jehoiakim, 183, 185.
Jehovah, 211.
Jeremiah, 184, 186-7, 189.
Jeroboam, 150, 158, 160.
Jerusalem, 80, 102, 115, 117, 119, 159, 184, 186, 193, 194, 200, 211-2, 222.
Jesus, 199, 210.
Jethro, 129.
Joab, 149.
Jochanan, 197, 199.
Joppa, 123.
Jordan, 127.
Joseph, 61, 73, 74, 79, 82, 83, 92, 93, 94, 95, 97.
Joseph-el, 110 n.
Josephus, 188, 199, 211, 212, 215, 219, 221.
Joshua, 75, 76, 118, 119.
Josiah, 182, 192, 194.
Judah (person), 79.
Judah (kingdom), 158-9, 160-1, 163, 165, 175, 182, 184, 185, 186.
Judea, 210.
Judges, the, 121-2.

Kadesh, 80, 107, 128, 129, 130, 131.
Kames, 71, 72.
Karbanit, 178.

Karnak, 160.
Keheret, 135-6.
Kemwer, 163.
Keturah, 20.
Khabiru, 75, 76, 77, 115 ff.
Khammurabi, 28, 49-53.
Khananiah, 204-5.
Khnemhotp, tomb of, 60.
Khnum, 196, 202.
Kishon, 162.
Klysma, 133.
Kudur-lagamar, 51.
Kudur-mabuk, 50.
Kue, 155-6-7.
Kush, 159, 165.
Kushi, 173.
Kushim, 159, 165.

Lagamar, 51.
Lagides, 209.
Land tenure in Egypt, 95-7.
Larsa, 50-51.
Lebanon, 112, 168.
Leontopolis, 212, 213-4-5-6.
Leyden Papyri, 123.
Libya, 109.
Libyans, 148, 159, 165, 169.
Lot, 53.
Lubim, 179.
Lubims, 159.
Luxor, 70.

Maccabees, 211.
Madyan, 129.
Magdola, 87.
Magdolo, 141.
Magdolus, 182.
Magicians, 92.
Mahseiah, 204.
Malkatu, 59.
Manetho, 25, 41, 45, 67-9.
Marah, 131-2-3.
Marea, 190.
Mareshah, 164, 166.
Maryn, 124.
Medes, 181, 183.
Megiddo, 182.
Melukhkha, 173-4.
Memphis, 68, 80, 141, 177-8, 189, 212, 215.
Menakhem, 208.
Menelaus, 210.

Menes, 37.
Menmare, 142.
Menthu, 40.
Mentuhotp, son of Hapi, 95.
Merenptah, 65, 76, 78, 82, 88, 107-10, 112, 120-1.
Meribath-Kadesh, 128.
Merykere, King, 38.
Mesopotamia, 49.
Mibhtahyah, 204.
Midianites, 129-130.
Migdol, 132, 135-6, 140-3, 189.
Milcah, 59.
Mitanni, 151.
Mizraim, 155-6, 172.
Modiana, 129.
Moon-god, 59.
Moses, 22, 84-5, 93, 129.
Mound of Onias (so-called), 219.
Mummification, 93.
Musri, 156-7, 168, 170-5.
Myth, nature of, 13 ff.

Nabopolassar, 184.
Naharina, 183.
Napata, 169, 172, 178.
Naram-sin, 56.
Nebat, 158.
Nebuchadnezzar, 80, 184, 186-7-8.
Necho, 178, 180-4.
Neferhotp, 60.
Nehemiah, 191, 199, 200.
Neit, 101.
Nephayan, 196.
Nesubanebded, 148.
Nile, 79, 87.
Nineveh, 174, 178, 184.
Nisin, Dynasty of, 57.
No-amon, 179.
Noph, 189.
Nubia, 159, 178.

On, 97.
Onias III, 210, 211.
Onias IV, 211 ff.
Osorkon I, 164.
Osorkon III, 169.
Ostanes, 197, 200.

P, Document, 26, 27, 32, 132-3, 137.
Padan-aram, 118.

Palestine, 69, 112, 114, 117-8, 121, 164, 167.
Paran, 127-9.
Passover, 15, 205, 224-6.
Pathros, 189, 190-1.
Paulinus, 212.
Pelusiac Nile, 69.
Pelusin, 86.
Pelusium, 69, 85, 86, 90, 137-40, 142-3, 176.
Persia, 50, 52, 80.
Persians, 190-1.
Petrograd papyri, 38, 53, 56.
Pharaoh, meaning of, 103.
Philistia, 181.
Philistines, 150, 153, 158, 163, 168, 175
Philistines, Way of the, 137-8.
Phoenicia, 168, 185.
Phoenician fleet, 178.
Piankhi, 169, 172-3.
Pi-hahiroth, 132, 135-6, 140, 143.
Pi-keheret, 135-6.
Pi-Ramessu, 85, 90, 137.
Pir'u (Pharaoh), 171, 173.
Pisebkhanu II, 150, 152.
Pi-Sopd, 81.
Pithom, 65, 77, 80, 82-4 n, 85-6, 90, 99, 108, 134-5.
Pithom stela, 135.
Pi-Tum, 86, 87, 90.
Plagues, 15, 48, 93.
Popilius, 210.
Potiphar, 92, 100.
Poti-pherah, 97, 98, 100, 101.
Predynastic Period, 37.
Priests, Egyptian, 97.
Proper names, Egyptian, 100 ff.
Psammetichus I, 181, 187.
Psammetichus II, 185, 192, 214.
Ptolemy, 210.
Ptolemy I, 209.
Ptolemy II, 34.
Ptolemy Philadelphus, 135.
Ptolemy Philometor, 211.
Ptolemy Soter II, 224.
Put, 179.

Qarqar, Battle of, 54, 111, 156, 168.
Qasr Bint el-Yahudi, 216.
Quails, 137 n.

Ra, 70, 98, 100, 101.

Raamses, see Rameses.
Rafa, 138.
Rameses (town or land), 77, 78, 80, 82 ff, 108, 120, 134, 137-8.
Ramesses II, 83, 84 *n*, 108-9, 110, 111, 120, 121, 123, 147, 148, 151.
Ramesses III, 83, 121, 124.
Ramesses IV, 124.
Ramesses XII, 147.
Raphia, 170.
Rebekah, 118.
Red Sea, 79, 87, 107, 132, 135, 137, 144.
Rehoboam, 154, 158, 163, 166.
Reuben, tribe of, 107 *n*.
Riblah, 183, 186.
Rim Sin, 51.

Sabaka, see Shabaka.
Saft el-Henneh, 81.
Sagaz, 116, 117.
Sais, 178.
Sakere, 146.
Salatis, King, 68.
Sallier I, Papyrus, 70.
Sallier IV, Papyrus, 140.
Samaria, 80, 169, 170, 172, 194, 200.
Samaritan transcript, 26, 27, 34, 75.
Sanballat, 200, 201.
Saqqara, 215.
Sarah, 59.
Sargon, 56, 170, 174.
Scythians, 181.
Sea of Reeds, 131, 132, 136, 137, 143-5.
Seb'e, see So.
Sebek-khu, 39-40, 62.
Seir, 115, 128, 129.
Sekhet, 214 *n*.
Sekhmet, 214.
Sekmem, 40, 62.
Sele, 141.
Seleucus, 209.
Selua, 208.
Semitic migrations, 56, 66-7, 118.
Sennacherib, 174-5-6.
Senusret II, 61.
Senusret III, 44.
Septuagint, 26-7, 34, 75, 79, 83, 156, 159.
Seqenenre, 70, 71, 72.
Seqenenre III, 94.
Serapeum, 135.

Serapiu, 135.
Serbonis, Lake, 138.
Set, 70, 98.
Sethet, 40.
Seti I, 110-11, 121, 142-3, 147.
Seve, see So.
Sev'e, see So.
Shabaka, 169, 171, 172, 174, 176.
Shabaku, see Shabaka.
Shabtai, 223.
Shallum, 208.
Shalmaneser, 170.
Shalmaneser II, 156.
Sharratu, 59.
Sharuhen, 69, 73.
Shechem, 40.
Shelemiah, 198, 200.
Shepherd Kings, 69.
shesh, meaning of, 103.
Sheshonk I, 152, 154, 158 ff.
Shinar, 49.
Shishak, see Sheshonk I.
Shur, 127.
Siamon, 150, 152.
Sib'i, 170-1.
Sidon, 177.
Sin (deity), 58, 59.
Sin (wilderness), 127.
Sinai, 31.
Sinai, Mount, 58, 126, 128, 129, 130.
Sinai, Peninsula of, 127, 130, 131, 133.
Sinai (wilderness), 127.
Sin-uballit, 199, 200.
Sinuhe, 38.
Sirius, 42.
So, 170-3.
Soa, see So.
Solomon, 28, 54, 111-2, 149-58.
Sothic Cycle, 43-4.
Sothic Period, 43.
Sothis, 42-3.
Store-cities, 83, 108.
Straw in bricks, 99.
Succoth, 77, 83, 88-9, 132, 134-5, 139, 143.
Suez Canal, 79.
Suez, Gulf of, 132.
Sukiims, 159.
Sumeria, 17.
Sun's Disk, 113, 146.
Sutekh, 70.
Syene, 141, 190, 196.

Syncellus, 25.
Syria, 57, 61-2, 109-10, 112, 114, 117, 119, 121, 148, 156, 167-8, 180, 209.
Syriac version, 34.
Syrians, 160.

Tahpanes, 80, 149.
Tahpanhes, 186-7.
Tanis, 80, 86, 148, 176.
Tanutamon, 180.
Targum of Palestine, 86.
Taylor Prism, 175.
Tell Balamun, 179 n.
Tell Defenneh, 216.
Tell el-Amarna, 113.
Tell el-Amarna letters, 75, 76, 144 ff., 151.
Tell el-Her, 142-3.
Tell el-Maskhuteh, 86, 87, 88, 142.
Tell el-Yahudiyeh, 69, 213, 215-6, 223.
Tell er-Retabeh, 83, 87-8, 90.
Tell Yahud, 216.
Teman, 129.
Temple of Onias (supposed), 218 ff.
Temple of Solomon 28, 54, 111, 151-2, 220, 221.
Textual corruption, 25-6, 33-4.
Thebes, 70-2, 146, 169, 177-8, 180.
Theker-baal, 148.
Thekoue, 156.
Theku, 65-6, 82-3, 87-9, 134, 139, 142-3.
Thel, 138, 139, 141, 142-3.
Thothmes III, 112, 146.
Thothmes IV, 113.
Tidal, 49, 51.
Tiglath-pileser IV, 168.
Timaios, King, 67.
Timsah, Lake, 135.
Tirhakah, 175-8.
Titus, 213.
Troglodutai, 159
Trogodutai, 159.
Tum, 83, 86.
Turin Papyrus of Kings, 45.

Tut-ankh-amon, 146.
Tut-ankh-aton, 146.
Ty, Queen, 113.
Tyre, 177.

UR, 57-9.

VENUS, 53.
Vulgate, 34.

WADI GHARANDEL, 133.
Wadi Tumilat, 65, 66, 79, 80, 81, 82, 83, 85, 86, 87, 89, 132, 134, 136.
Wall of the Prince, 38.
Warad Sin, 50-51.
Wenamon, 148.
Widarnag, 196.
Wilderness, wanderings in, 107, 127.

XERXES, 191.

YADHAMELEK, 162.
Yahu (Yahweh), 193 ff.
Yahweh, 22, 31, 106, 122, 128, 129, 130, 202.
Yamani, 173-4.
Ya-u (deity), 58.
Yeb, 190 ff.
Yedoniah, 193, 196, 198, 205, 208.
Yeho, 58.
Yenoam, 109.
ye'ōr, meaning of, 103.
Yo, 58.

ZAPHENATHPANEAH, 100-1.
Zare, 164.
Zedekiah, 185-6.
Zephathah, 164.
Zerah, 163-6.
Zerubbabel, 222-3.
Zeus, 211.
Zin, 127.
Zoan, 86.
Zoan, Field of, 86.
Zoroaster, 204.

Made and Printed in Great Britain by C. TINLING & Co., LTD.,
53, Victoria Street Liverpool,
and at London and Prescot.

TELEPEN

UNIVERSITY OF NOTTINGHAM

6 00 221252 X

WITHDRAWN

FROM THE LIBRARY